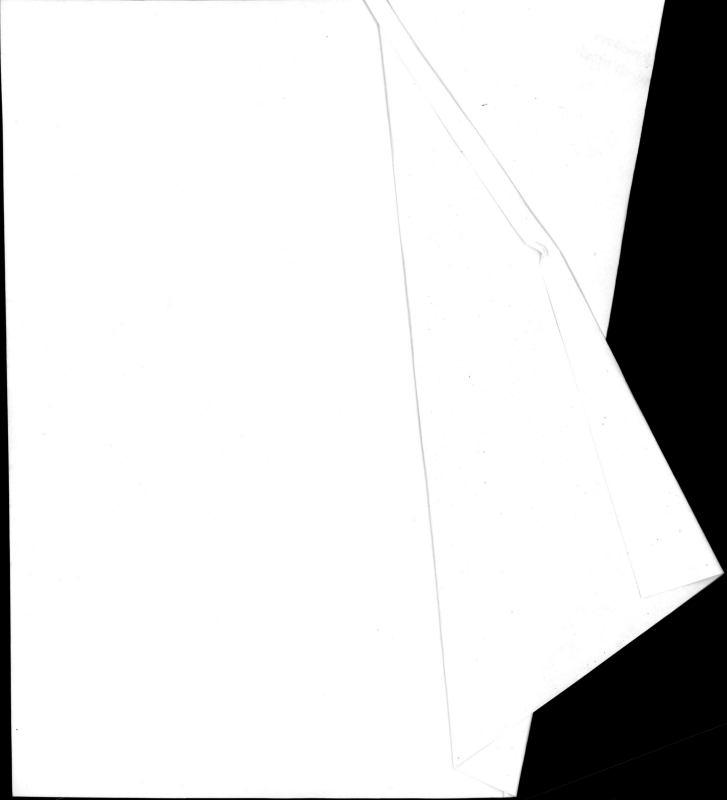

FIGHTER FOR FREEDOM
MAHARAJA DULEEP SINGH

Editor
Dr. Baldev Singh Baddan

NATIONAL BOOK SHOP
Pleasure Garden Market,
Chandni Chowk, Delhi-110006

© N B Shop, Delhi 2007

ISBN 81-7116-210-X

Rs. 175/-

Published by
National Book Shop
Pleasure Garden Market,
Chandni Chowk, Delhi-110006

Lasertypeset at
Word & Graphics
Jatwara, Darya Ganj, New Delhi-110 002

Printed at
Avon Offset Printers
Darya Ganj, New Delhi-110 002

CONTENTS

Ever affectionately
Dulup Singh

INTRODUCTION

History, by and large, has painted Maharaja Duleep Singh as a thorough English country gentleman of his times, living beyond his means and incurring debts in consequence. Living in London after his exile to England, he spent most of his youth in his favourite pastimes of fencing, hawking, hunting and shooting.

And yet for all his spirited exertions in later life to free his motherland from the British yoke and regain his sovereignty having come to nought, he is seen as a pathetic, helpless figure, an object of pity and in British eyes an object of ridicule. G.B. Mallesan in his introduction to 'Lady Login's Recollections' in the following pages has succinctly shown the two facets of the Maharaja when he recalls that the Maharaja had confessed to him in 1871 that he had had a thrilling and thoroughly satisfying life for over 17 years of his stay in England (he had come in 1854 at the age of 16) and reckoned himself the happiest man on earth. But just ten years later when Col. Mallesan again chanced to meet him, the Maharaja told him that he was the most miserable man that there ever lived. What had happened in the intervening period to impair his perfect happiness of long standing into utter despair? He died in 1893, at the age of 55, an exhausted, shattered and broken-hearted man.

Let me lope through history of the period to highlight the reasons that had contributed to the early happiness and later despair of Maharaja Duleep Singh.

Maharaja Ranjit Singh died on June 27, 1839; his eldest son, Kharak Singh whom Ranjit Singh had himself appointed his successor, succeeded to the throne. He had hardly been on the throne for three months, when he was dethroned in favour of his son Naunihal Singh. Few days later Kharak Singh died, allegedly by slow poisoning that was seen as the handiwork of the Minister Dhyan Singh, who was the lead player in the tragic drama that unfolded after Ranjit Singh's death.

7

This was first of the assassinations during the period between Ranjit Singh's death and annexation of Punjab, a period marked by assassinations, conspiracies, treacheries, betrayals and wars. Three Maharajas, three princes, three vazirs and two of the principle Sardars were killed during this decade of intense turbulence that saw the end of Sikh rule in Punjab.

On the day Maharaja Kharak Singh was cremated, his son and successor, Maharaja Naunihal Singh, was killed in an accident which some insiders suspected was a deftly executed murder.

Maharani Chand Kaur, mother of Maharaja Naunihal Singh, was crowned Maharani on 8th November, 1840 but was dethroned in favour of Maharaja Sher Singh, a son of Maharaja Ranjit Singh. The Maharani was later murdered on 13th June, 1842.

Maharaja Sher Singh was crowned on 18th January, 1841 A.D. and was murdered on 15th September, 1843. He ruled for a little over two and a half years.

Tikka Pertap Singh, son of Maharaja Sher Singh, barely 8 years old, was also murdered along with his father on 15th September, 1843.

A series of murders of Ministers, Sardars and courtiers of the Sikh Raj characterise the period immediately after the death of Maharaja Ranjit Singh.

Sardars Chet Singh, adviser of Maharaja Kharak Singh, was murdered on 8th October, 1839; Raja Dhyan Singh, Minister, on 15th September, 1843; Lehna Singh Sandhanwalia on 15th September, 1843; Sardar Ajit Singh Sandhanwalia, Giani Gurmukh Singh, Misr Beli Ram on 15th September, 1843; Chet Singh Dogra (brother of Raja Gulab Singh and Raja Dhyan Singh) was murdered, by his nephew Hira Singh on 27th March, 1844, who in turn was murdered on 21st December, 1844; Prince Kashmira Singh (a son of Maharaja Ranjit Singh), Sant Baba Bir Singh, S. Attar Singh Sandhanwalia on 7th May, 1844; Pt. Jalla, Mian Labh Singh, Mian Sohan Singh on 21st December, 1844; Kanwar Pishora Singh (another son of Maharaja Ranjit Singh) on 30th August, 1845 and Minister Jawahar Singh on 21st December 1845.

Maharaja Duleep Singh was the youngest son of Maharaja Ranjit Singh and last of the most eligible successors to the throne. He was born on 5th September, 1838 and was crowned on 15th September,

8

1843 at the age of five and dethroned by the British following annexation of Punjab to British dominions on 29th March, 1849. He ruled for a little over five and a half years making his rule the longest among the successors of Maharaja Ranjit Singh. He was the only surviving son of Maharaja Ranjit Singh at the time of the annexation of Punjab which was just about a decade after the great Maharaja's death in 1839.

There was a definite threat to Maharaja Duleep Singh's life too but the plot was discovered well in time and nipped in the bud by his mother Rani Jindan who was her Regent. There would have been many more plots to kill him judging from the fact that conspirators and killers were still continuing to run amok with no check or hindrance whatsoever. It was not until the first Anglo-Sikh war when the Sikhs lost and Punjab came under British protection and administration under Bhyrowal Treaty that the killing spree ended. Under the Bhyrowal Treaty of 1846, article VII states, "A British force of such strength and numbers, and in such positions as the Governor-General may think fit, shall remain at Lahore for the protection of the Maharaja and the preservation of the peace of the country."

The British did preserve peace in the country, and provided protection to the Maharaja such that he could survive the massacre of the royalty and nobility that had been an on-going operation after Maharaja Ranjit Singh's death. The British also preserved the infant Maharaja's sovereignty until 1848 when following the Second Anglo-Sikh war Punjab was finally annexed and Maharaja Duleep Singh was deposed. He was yet accorded high-degree security as ward of the British Government till he was of the age of majority when he was removed from Punjab altogether to live a peaceful and contented life in England on a maintenance allowance considered good enough then to afford the Maharaja a life-style befitting his status.

The Maharaja, according to his gaurdian Dr. Login, was quite intelligent and smart for his age. It is not improbable that the Maharaja carried childhood impressions well into manhood. The impressions of the events around him when he was yet an infant were certainly not happy ones. They must have been stinging him and tormenting him throughout his life. Even as a child-ruler with a retinue of protection force around him he could never feel secure, especially after he saw his own uncle, and his Minister, Jawahar Singh, getting slaughtered before his own eyes and his helpless mother who was her regent and was by his side at that time could do no more than wail and beat her chest at the hacked body of her brother. He himself was snatched away from his mother and confined in a secluded place for a brief while.

With a background of unholy events and uneasy impressions of his palace life and career in Lahore as an infant sovereign, the opportunity to have a contented and peaceful life of a country gentleman in a far-away place like London must have been a matter of good fortune. It must have taken little or nothing to persuade the Maharaja to abjure his faith whose uncivilty and barbarity he had seen enough in his infancy. He, it is claimed, converted to Christianity of his own free will. He had experienced Christian love and charity and was highly impressed, especially in contrast to the uncivilty and barbarity he had seen and known in the setting of the Sikh faith and society. After conversion he soon established himself in the peace and tranquility that his adopted faith held out to him. It was then that G.B. Mallesan had found him boast that he was the "happiest man on earth." He was grateful to the British that they had rescued him well in time from the bloodthirsty hounds whose master he was supposed to be and whose next and the last important victim he himself most possibily was. He was grateful to the British that after rescuing him thus they had set him up on a new course of life, in a new location, which appeared to be more civilised and satisfying. He was happy to be a loyal subject of the crown and fortunate to be blue-eyed boy of Queen Victoria.

Not until he had begun to have pecuniary problems inevitable in the midst of fast moving city life and growing demands of an expanding family that he undertook to introspect and have a second look at his own history and situation. He read the available literature on the history of Punjab. He read the blue book and discovered ruefully that he had been cheated out of his kingdom by the crafty British. The two treaties the British had him to sign when he was yet an infant could not after all be taken on their face value. The British continue to be anxious to see him removed far away from his land and people who once were under his lordship; away from his mother who they identify as a scheming monster; away from even legitimate opulance for they fear it might lend him power to disturb their equnimity. It was in such a frame of mind—turbulent and rebellious—that G.b. Mallesan, happened to meet the Maharaja once again and found him this time the most miserable man that ever lived on this earth.

In the book in hand, we have included some parts of the most important of writings on Duleep Singh, "Lady Login's Recollections" based on Dr. Login's correspondence with his wife and stores of documents left by him in her possession. The great merit of the narrative is that it tells "the truth, the whole truth and nothing but the truth." Lady Login, though not happy with Duleep Singh for turning against his benefactors, gives a generous revelation of the causes which had influenced the Maharaja in turning against the British—from complete loyalty to the crown to outright rebellion against its connection.

The articles "Rebellious Maharaja" and "Maharaja, the crusader" included in this volume correctly portray the rebellious facet of Duleep Singh's character in his new avatar. The then Lt. Governor of Punjab writing to the Viceroy Marquis of Rippon referred to Duleep Singh as the "Injured representative of the Lahore family". Writes Secretary of State in a telegram to Viceroy on 31st March 1886: "In recent communication with Political Secretary (Sir Own Burne) he (Maharaja) has used language of menacing character; referring to eventual troubles in India, war with Russia and the part he may take as head of the nation. An address from him is stated to have been sent to India, just published in newspapers. It announces his intention to be rebaptised into Sikh faith with a view to take his blessings as Guru of the nation. Maharaja announces steps by which he is to be restored to power... Affairs if neglected might possibly give serious trouble. He is in a new state of mind which seems to border on mono-mania."

How the Maharaja has been seen by the non-Punjabi historians is the subject matter of Himadri Bannerjee's "Maharaja Duleep Singh in the Eyes of Non-Sikhs". An important landmark in the development of Bengali historiography of the Sikhs was the publication of *Sikh Judder Itihas O Maharaja Duleep Singh* in 1893. The author of the monograph, Barodakanta Mitra, reviews Sikh history of the period with reference to the life and career of Maharaja Duleep Singh highlighting particularly the influence his mother had in shaping his patriotic thought. Thirty years after Mitra's publication came another monograph

11

from Calcutta, this time in Hindi, by Nandkumardev Sharma under the title *Punjab Haran aur Maharaja Duleep Singh* (1921). His studies carry a deep patriotic sentiment. Incidently those were the times when the Akalis were agitating for Gurdwara reforms and Punjab had witnessed Rowlatt Satyagrah and Jallianbagh massacre. Mahatma Gandhi had launched non-cooperation movement against the British for Swaraj. Sharma's monograph reflected anti-British sentiment through Duleep Singh's struggle against the British in India. Sharma's Duleep Singh was a fighter for freedom. The Maharaja's crusade represents early phase of India's freedom struggle.

Dr. Kirpal Singh ("Maharaja's visit to Russia as Viewed by British Government") discovers a bunch of private letters between Lord Cross who was home secretary during 1886-87 in Lord Dissrali's cabinet and Lord Dufferin Governor-General in India. The letters throw light on the activity of British Intelligence Service that had been dogging Maharaja Duleep Singh throughout the period 1886-87 when the Maharaja sneaked into Russia in disguise. The Maharaja's personal attendant, Watson, was planted on him by the British Government. The correspondence which had not been officially made public before throw a flood of light on the British effort to frustrate the Maharaja's bid to enlist Russian support for the freedom of the country.

Numismatics, the study of coins, has been considered a help-maid of history. It has been used to ascertain historical facts, to understand the influence of rulers at different times and at different places. Gurpreet Singh's "Coinage during the Period of Maharaja Duleep Singh" gives details of the seven mints that had been at work during the period of Sikh rule. Of the mints, Namak-Shahi mint is considered the most important as far as Maharaja Duleep Singh's period is concerned. Its location has been somewhere in the salt-ranges, hence the name Namak Shahi. It struck silver rupees of the years 1847 and 1848 and seems to be the product of rebellious proceedings then going on in certain parts of Punjab.

This volume should provide interesting reading to all those interested in the history of India's freedom movement for Maharaja Duleep Singh is now seen as one of the early and most important freedom fighters of India.

—S.P. Gulati

Chapter I

LADY LOGIN'S NARRATIVE

Introduction

A few lines which I wrote on the subject of Duleep Singh in the *Asiatic Quarterly* about a year ago (1888) procured for me the pleasure of an acquaintance with Lady Login, whom I found to be even more interested than myself in the conduct and treatment of one who had been her husband's ward in the tenderest and most impressionable years of his life. I soon found that whilst Lady Login regretted equally with myself the wayward conduct of the Maharajah since he quitted England, we both agreed that there were many circumstances in his history, a knowledge of which would induce a public which judged only from facts within its ken to take a more lenient, or, at all events, a less prejudiced view of conduct which, without such explanation, would appear wholly unjustifiable. No living being was so thoroughly acquainted with all the circumstances attending the Maharajah's youth, early training, development into manhood, and subsequent career as Lady Login; nor could any one tell as accurately the history of those monetary relations towards the Government which has influenced so unfortunately the later actions of the Maharajah.

I respectfully urged, then, upon Lady Login in the advisability, in the interests of the Maharajah, in the interests of truth and justice, of writing from the stores of documents in her possession a connected history of the Maharajah's life, from the date of the connection with him of the late Sir John Login to the time of the cessation of that connection. The story might, I ventured to suggest, form one of the main features of the life of one of the noblest servants of the late East India Company—Sir John Login himself.

The idea commended itself to Lady Login, and she at once acted

13

upon it. How admirably Lady Login has performed the self-allotted task the public, I am confident, will unhesitatingly admit. The great merit of the Lady Login's narrative is that it tells "the truth, the whole truth, and nothing but the truth." Lady Login has kept back nothing that she was able to tell. The result is a valuable contribution to contemporary history, and, what is of not less importance, a complete revelation of the causes which have influenced Duleep Singh in his hostility towards the British Government.

I have myself always held that the treatment dealt out to Duleep Singh after the close of the second Sikh war was alike impolitic and unjust. When that war broke out Duleep Singh was the ward of the British Government. He was a child of nine years old, and took no part whatever in the administration of the country of which the British Government had recognized him to be the Sovereign, but of which the English Resident and a council of native nobles were the actual rulers. The revolt of Moolraj, and the outbreak of Sikh chieftains in the Hazarah which followed that revolt, were directed against the actual Government of Lahore, which, as I have said, was presided over by an English Resident, and which ruled in the name of the Duleep Singh. Yet, when those risings were suppressed on the field of Gujarat, the British Government, then absolute master of the situation, visited the sins of Moolraj and the Hazarah chiefs on their innocent ward, deprived him of his kingdom, and he has always asserted—though this would seem to be denied—of the estates which his father had accumulated, and consigned him to the care of Doctor—afterwards Sir John—Login.

To a truer-hearted, more conscientious, or better man it would have been impossible to consign him. How thoroughly and how well Sir John, aided in every particular by Lady Login, performed his duty towards the young Prince is admirably told in these pages. Upon this part of the history I do not propose to dwell in this Introduction. There can be no doubt—indeed, I had it from the Maharajah's own lips in 1871—that throughout this period, and at the date also of his speaking to me on the subject, he was thoroughly happy. I propose, rather, to ask the attention of the reader to the circumstances related in the chapter "Duleep Singh and the Government 1856-86" —circumstances which explain the sudden migration from happiness to discontent, from discontent to despair, from despair to acts bordering on insanity.

14

It would seem that the Maharajah was a man of a trustful, generous and open disposition. Further, that he did not care to bother himself with details, and that he hated business matters. So long as Sir John Login lived he was happy. Though often urged to effect a settlement, or rather to insist that the India Office should make a definite settlement with him, he always put it off. He was content to have Sir John between him and the India Office. After Sir John's death, Colonel Oliphant, whom he appointed equerry and controller of his household, soon gained an ascendency which produced similar feelings of trust. He was then living at Elveden, where he had the best shooting in England; and when I stayed with him there in 1871, he told me he was the happiest man in the world. When I next saw him, about ten years ago (1879), he told me he was the most miserable. His words were to the effect that subsequently to Colonel Oliphant's death he had discovered that he had been cheated out of his kingdom, and out of the private estates which his father had possessed, and that he could get no settlement from the India office; that he had still hopes that he might ultimately succeed, but that the treatment he had received had well-nigh broken his heart. He complained bitterly that no provision had been made for his family. When at Elveden, he said, he was in constant hope that he might receive an English title, and with that title such a sum attached to it inalienably as might make him forget that he had ever sat on the footsteps of a throne; which hope, he added, was growing dimmer and dimmer, till it was well-nigh extinguished. He told me this one evening, the only evening that I dined with him, at the Garrick Club, of which he was a member. The time, to the best of my recollection, was 1879-80.

The evil, as Lady Login tells us, dates from the time of the annexation of the Punjab. No settlement, properly so called, was then made. But, when Duleep Singh attained his majority, Sir John Login pressed upon Sir Charles Wood the necessity of coming to a settlement on the terms of the Treaty, and suggested Sir John Lawrence as the most suitable person to draw up the agreement. Sir Charles Wood, after some delay, assented; and Sir John Lawrence agreed to act in the matter on condition that Sir Frederick Currie should be associated with him. This was conceded. The two men met and drew up a report. This report, however, was objected to in Council, and was never acted upon.

The outcome was that somewhat later Sir Charles Wood offered "improved" terms to Duleep Singh. The Maharajah accepted these terms, with the reservation of his rights, as the head of the family, of being allowed to have a voice in the apportioning of the fund known as the "Five Lakh Fund," and to inspect the account. He further claimed the repayment of his losses in the Mutiny. This was the last transaction. It occurred just before Sir John Login's death.

It is to be regretted that the Indian Council set aside the settlement proposed by Sir John Lawrence and Sir Frederick Currie. These men had been on the spot; they knew all the circumstances of his case; and if their recommendations had been attended to, Duleep Singh would still be a loyal subject of the Queen, and the "perfect happiness" of 1871 would never have been impaired. But not only was the recommendations not acted upon, but no permanent settlement was ever arrived at. The relation between the Maharajah and the India Office can be best described as having been from first to last hand-to-mouth relations.

As a specimen of what these have occasionally been, I quote Lady Login: "The Government has never accounted to the Maharajah for the money received for the sale of the house, nor has he received anything in respect of the value of the land, though the papers show that the whole was purchased out of his money; nor any compensation in respect of the contents of the house which were destroyed at the Mutiny." Lady Login proceeds to show that during thirty years differences arose which would have instantly disappeared if the recommendations to which I have referred had been adopted. Since then officials have arisen who had had no part in the original treaty—who knew nothing of Duleep Singh as the recognized ruler of a powerful state—who knew him only as a deposed prince, asking, as they considered it, for alms.

The Maharajah, doubtless, has many faults, and his more recent conduct requires the exercise of a large amount of charity. But there are few who will rise from the perusal of Lady Login's account without admitting that he has suffered great wrongs, and without asking whether it is yet too late, by a generous concession, to bring back the lost sheep to the fold he quitted in despair.

G.B. MALLESON

July 12th, 1889   16

THE SIKHS

The Punjab, or Land of the "Five Rivers,"[1] was first known to Western nations as the kingdom of Porus. The Greeks under Alexander, who defeated that monarch, gave to the country he ruled over the name of "India." This name in later ages extended to those vast territories which lie betwixt the Indus and the Irrawaddy, and stretch from Cape Comorin to the farthest Himalayas.

The Punjab itself is about the size of the present kingdom of Prussia (including Hanover and Schleswig-Holstein), though its population is not quite so dense as that of northern Germany.[2] It enjoys every variety of climate, from the drifting snows of Ladakh to the dust-storms of Mooltan.[3] The products of the soil are equally varied, and though it is not so marvellously fertile as parts of Bengal and the basin of the Ganges, even in the days of Runjeet Singh the revenues were estimated at two and a half millions sterling, while under British rule they have nearly doubled.[4] The wealth of the country, however, is largely owing to its trade in shawls, carpets, and silk goods (the shawls of Cashmere and carpets of Mooltan being almost equally famous), and to its export of salt—the salt mines of the Jhelum district forming a valuable source of revenue to the British Government.

The inhabitants are of many races, the most numerous in the central plain, about the cities of Lahore and Amritsur, being the Jats— a tribe of Central Asian origin—and it was amongst these people that the Sikh theism had its birth.

It must not be forgotten that the Sikhs in origin were a *religious body*, and not a *race*. They were banded together, not by the ties of kindred or common ancestry, but by the ardour and religious zeal of one earnest soul searching for Divine truth, who formed them into a brotherhood of enthusiastic disciples, sworn to carry on his mission to succeeding generations, and bring all who accept their teaching of whatever tribe, language, or religion, from the darkness of idolatry and debased superstition, which disgraced all the creeds of India, to the simple worship of the one Supreme Deity. Unlike the followers of Mohammad, the Sikhs made no converts by the sword.

Nanak, the founder of the Sikh religion, was born in the year 1469. The Adi Granth, or sacred book of the Sikhs, which contains his

17

writings, show that the doctrines he taught breathe a high spirituality and truely exalted moral character. Here and there, indeed, they bear a strange and shadowy resemblance to some of the precepts of the Christian faith. Nanak taught that God was One, Eternal, Incomprehensible, the Creator of all; that *all* creeds were to be tolerated, and *all* founders of religious systems honoured as teachers sent to reveal some portion of Divine truth; but they were on no account to be regarded as deities themselves. The Hindu religion and that of Mohammed is thus placed on equal terms.

Nanak was succeeded by nine Gurus or teachers, whereof Govind[5] was the tenth and last. Govind proclaimed the foundation of the Khalsa[6] or sacred commonwealth of the Sikhs. Caste was to be done away, and all Sikhs were equally to receive the *pahul*, or initiatory rite;[7] the locks of the faithful were to remain unshorn, and they were told to assume the surname of "Singh" (lion).

Govind also formed the Sikhs into a military and political organization, and when he died, in 1708, told his followers that the mission of the appointed "Ten" was fulfilled; and henceforth the Guruship was absorbed in the general body of the Khalsa.

Politically the Sikhs were divided into a number of separate "Misls" or confederacies, each headed by a Sirdar or chief. These associations are peculiarly Sikh institutions, and the name being derived from an Arabic word signifying "alike or equal," implies that they were associations of *equals*, under chiefs of their own selection. The Sirdar's portion being first divided off, the remainder of the lands and property acquired by these bands of freebooters was parcelled out among his followers—whether relatives, friends, volunteers, or hired retainers— who had followed his banner in the field, and who each took his part as co-sharer, and held it in absolute independence.[8]

It is in the year 1762 that the name of Charrut Singh, Chief of the Sooker-Chukea Misl, first rises into notice, he having then established a stronghold in his wife's village of Goojranwallah, famous in after years as the birth-place of his grandson, the renowned Ranjeet Singh.

When, in 1774, Charrut Singh was killed by the bursting of his own matchlock, and was succeeded in his chieftainship by his son,

Maha Singh, the revenues of his Misl were estimated at three lakhs of rupees (£30,000).[9]

Maha Singh overthrew and slew Jai Singh, the chief of the Kuneia Misl, who had become the most powerful amongst the Sikh Sirdars, and married the infant grand-daughter of Jai Singh to his only son Ranjeet Singh. That youth, therefore, on his father's death, in 1792, found himself, at the early age of twelve years, paramount chief of the Sikh nation.

In the year 1799, in return for services rendered to the Afghan Shah Zuman, Ranjeet Singh received a royal investiture of the city of Lahore. Thus was the first step gained towards the establishing of kingly power in the Punjab, though it was not until ten years later, that his predominance over the other Sirdars was firmly fixed, and a formal treaty entered into with the British (April 25th, 1809), in which he was acknowledged as ruler of all the Sikhs (except those of Malwa and Sirhind, south of the Sutlej, which were under British protection), and whereby perpetual friendship was secured between the British Government and the State of Lahore—an engagement faithfully kept throughout his life by the Maharajah.

Ranjeet Singh left at his death (June 27th, 1839) six sons, of whom *four* were legitimate, or "acknowledged," viz., (1) Kharrack Singh, born 1802; (2) Shere Singh, born 1807; (3) Tara Singh, said to be twin-brother of Shere Singh; (4) Duleep Singh, born September 4th 1838.

There were also two illegitimate, or "adopted," sons, viz., Cashmera Singh, born 1819; and Peshawura Singh, born 1823.

Of the "legitimate" sons, born of his wives, only two, however, Kharrack Singh and Duleep Singh, were fully acknowledged as such by the Maharajah; Shere Singh and Tara Singh having always been supposed by him, and generally believed, to have been substituted for a daughter by his first, or principal, wife, Mehtab Kaur, daughter of Gurbuksh Singh, and heiress of the Kuneia chieftainship. To neither of them did the Maharajah ever show any parental affection.[10] Shere Singh was commonly reported to be the son of a carpenter, and Tara Singh that of a weaver.

Tragic Events

Ranjeet Singh was succeeded by his eldest son Kharrack Singh, whose reign lasted barely five and a half months. Kharrack Singh was of weak intellect and the government rested entirely in the hands of his son, Nao-Nehal Singh. This Prince conspired with the famous three "Jammu Brothers"[11] to murder one Cheit Singh, the favourite of the Maharajah, his father. The crime was perpetrated at daybreak on the 8th October, 1839, within a few paces of the terrified monarch, who himself died soon after (November 5th) prematurely old and careworn.

That same day retribution overtook Nao-Nehal Singh, for, as he was returning from the performance of the last rites of the funeral pyre of his father, the masonry of a gateway under which he was passing gave way, and he, together with the eldest son of Gulab Singh, who was at his side, was crushed under the ruins. The Jammu Rajahs were, of course, suspected of his death, and it is possible that self-preservation have been their motive, as they well knew that Nao-Nehal Singh had determined on their destruction.[12]

For sometime the government was assumed by Chand Kaur, the widow of Kharrack Singh; but on the 18th January, 1841, through the influence of the Jammu Rajahs and the army, Shere Singh, the reputed son of Ranjeet Singh, was proclaimed Maharajah.

In 1843, Raja Dhyan Singh, who was Wazeer, finding that his influence with the Maharajah was on the wane, conspired with two Sirdars of the Sindhanwallah family,[13] named Ajeet Singh and Lena Singh, to murder both Shere Singh and his eldest son, Pertab Singh, a boy of thirteen or fourteen years. Dhyan Singh, however, gained little by his treachery, for he was murdered by his accomplices within an hour or two of his master. His death was avenged by his son, the youthful Heera Singh, who made an appeal to the army; and Ajeet Singh and Lena Singh were slain in their turn.[14]

Duleep Singh was then proclaimed Maharajah (September 18th, 1843), and Heera Singh raised to the "high and fatal office" of Wazeer.[15]

Duleep Singh was born in the palace of Lahore on the 4th September, 1838, about three months before the interview at Ferozepore between Lord Auckland and the rulers of the Sikhs, which preceded the advance of the army of the Indus to Afghanistan. He was at once acknowledged by the Maharajah Ranjeet Singh as his son, and much attention and kindness was shown to his mother, the Ranee Jinda, or Chunda. After the death of the "Great Maharajah," which occurred when the child was about ten months old, and during the reigns of Kharrack Singh and Shere Singh, the young prince continued to reside in the palace under his mother's care, receiving but little notice from either of his elder brothers, the reigning princes, or their ministers.

Since the death of Ranjeet Singh and the dissolution of the Misls, the army had been the real power in the State. Claiming to represent the Khalsa itself, it took upon it to discuss all national and important matters, and to have the selection of the occupant of the *guddee* (throne). It maintained a rigid internal discipline in itself, as far as military duties were concerned; but its relation to the Executive Government was determined by a council or assemblage of committees, composed of delegates from each battalion or regiment. These committees were termed "Panchayets," from the word *panch* (five), the mystic number of the Khalsa, and the system is a common one throughout Hindustan, where every section of a tribe or district has its panchayet, or village parliament.

The Maharanee Jinda was made Regent of her son. She was a woman of great capacity and strong will, who had considerable influence with the Panchayets, being a skillful intriguer and endowed with undoubted courage, though her moral character left much to be desired.

Dissensions soon broke out among the Jammu family. Suchet Singh, the youngest of the three "Jammu Brothers," was mortified at the ascendancy of his nephew, Heera Singh, and determined to supplant him. He broke at length into open rebellion, but was overthrown, and died, fighting to the last. Suchet Singh left no heirs, and his immense estates and wealth were the cause of much dispute later on. He had buried about one and a half million rupees' worth of treasure at Ferozepore on British territory, and this the Lahore Government claimed, both as escheated property of a feudatory without male heirs, and as the confiscated property of a rebel in arms, while the British Government contended that the claim must be pleaded and proved in a British court of justice.[16]

Rajah Gulab Singh had supported his nephew Heera Singh. He was the eldest and most crafty of the "Jammu Brothers"; his wealth and territories were enormous, and this overgrown vassal was a source of serious embarrassment to the central power. He was, however, reduced to submission by the army, and obliged to pay a fine of three and a half million rupees (£350,000), which was afterwards increased to six and three-quarter millions (£675,000).

Jawahir Singh, the brother of the Maharanee, was now ambitious of power. He conspired against Heera Singh, caused him to be put to death, and himself became Wazeer in his place; but falling under the displeasure of the Panchayets, was himself publicly shot by their order, in the presence of his sister and his nephew, the little Maharajah.

In the December of the same year (1845), the Sikh army crossed the Sutlej, and there followed what is known as the First Sikh War.

On the news reaching the capital, of the annihilation of his army at Sobraon, the young Maharajah set out for Kussoor, to offer his submission to the Governor General, Sir Henry Hardinge.[17] Some days later, at another durbar held at Lahore, Sir Henry asked to be allowed to see the famed Koh-i-noor. It was produced for his inspection, and afterwards passed round to the other Europeans present. Colonel Balcarres Ramsay thus describes the incident:

I arrived at the camp at Lahore, just as the Governor-General was going out with his *cortege* to meet the young Maharajah and receive his submission. There was a grand durbar afterwards, and when the Koh-i-noor was handed round for our inspection, Mr. Edwards, the Under-Secretary to Government in the Foreign Department, was put in charge of it. He was evidently extremely nervous, and carried it round himself from one staff officer to another. Just as he placed it in my hands, Sir Henry Hardinge sent for him; I naturally passed it on to the next officer, but when Edwards hurried back and demanded the precious jewel, I never shall forget the agony depicted on his face, as he rushed down the ranks of staff officers, frantically demanding it.[18]

Sir Henry then, with a pleasant smile, fastened it himself on the arm of the little King, afterwards patting him on the back in a kindly manner.[19]

Jullundur Doab Annexed

On the 20th February, 1846, the British troops entered Lahore, and the whole Punjab lay at their feet.[20] It was theirs by force of arms and the fortune of war, yet Sir Henry Hardinge had no thought of

22

annexation. He contented himself with annexing the Jullundur Doab, or country between the Sutlej and the Beas, and demanding an indemnity from the Lahore State of a crore and a half of rupees (one and a half million sterling). This sum the Lahore Treasury was unable to produce, and the Governor General took Cashmere and the Hill States, from the Beas to the Indus, in lieu of two-thirds of the indemnity, and transferred this territory to Rajah Golab Singh, as a separate sovereign, for a sum of one'million sterling. As, however, it was found advisable to retain a portion of this territory in the hands of the East India Company, this latter sum was reduced by one fourth, and the liquidation was rendered still more easy to the Jammu Prince, by considering him as heir to the money buried by his brother, Suchet Singh, at Ferozepore, and which was already in the possession of the East India Company.

Later on (March 11th), an additional clause was added to the Treaty, to the effect that a British force should remain at Lahore till the close of the year, to protect the Maharajah and his Government while the reorganization of the Khalsa army was in progress, but as the time approached when this force would be withdrawn, the uneasiness of the durbar, or council of ministers, prompted them to ask the Governor-General to continue to assist them in the administration of affairs, during the minority of the Maharajah, and the Treaty of Bhyrowal (December 16th, 1846) was the outcome of this request.[21] (See Appendix I)

Punjab under Despotic Rule

By this new Treaty, the Punjab was placed "under the dictatorship of a British Resident, who was to have full control over every department of the State. It provided for the continuance of a British force at Lahore until Maharajah Duleep Singh should attain the full age of sixteen, which would happen on the 4th September, 1854. The sum of twenty-two lakhs annually was to be paid by the Lahore State for the expenses of the occupation. The administration of the affairs of the country was to be continued, under the direction of the Resident, by a Council of Regency.....The Ranee was to be provided with a fitting maintenance, but was by this new arrangement to be virtually excluded from any share in the government.[22]

By the terms of the Treaty, the Resident was vested with

supreme and despotic powers, subject only to the instructions of the Governor-General.[23] In a letter dated 3rd July, 1847, Lord Hardinge reminds the Resident that the articles of government "give to the Government of India, represented at Lahore by its Resident, full power to direct and control all matters in every department of the State. It is politic", he says, "that the Resident should carry the native Council with him, the members of which are, however, entirely under his control and guidance; he can change them and appoint others; and in military affairs his powers are as unlimited as in the civil administration; he can withdraw Sikh garrisons, replacing them by British troops, in any and every part of the Punjab."[24] In a subsequent letter Lord Hardinge again urged on Henry Lawrence the advisability of keeping a tight hand on all native officials, and making his own personality felt in every department of the government.[25] The following extract from another letter of his will show what the real scope of the Treaty was, and that the Resident was to be entirely responsible for the administration of the country:-

October 23rd, 1847

In all our measures taken during the minority, we must bear in mind that by the Treaty of Lahore, March, 1846, the Punjab never was intended to be an independent State. By the clause, I added, the Chief of the State can neither make war nor peace, nor exchange nor sell an acre of territory, nor admit an European officer, nor refuse us a thoroughfare through his territories, nor, in fact, perform any act (except its own internal administration), without our permission. In fact, the native prince is in fetters, and under our protection, and must do our bidding. I advert hastily to this point because, if I have any difference of opinion with you, it consists in your liberality in attempting at too early a period to train the Sikh authorities to walk alone; I wish them to feel and to like our direct interference by the benefits conferred[26]

The Resident thus describes the practical working of the Council of Regency (August 1847) :-

On the whole, the durbar gives me as much support as I can reasonably expect; there has been a quiet struggle for mastery, but as, though I am polite to all, I allow nothing that appears to me wrong to pass unnoticed, the members of the Council are gradually falling into the proper train, and refer most questions to me, and, in words at least, allow, more fully even than I wish, that they are only executive officers—to do as they are bid.[27]

Although the Maharajah was too young to share the councils of those who ruled in his name, he was always present in state at the

24

durbars, and all dignities and honours were conferred by his hand.

It chanced that at a grand durbar held on the 7th August, 1847, it was arranged that distinctions should be given to various Sirdars who had rendered important services. Amongst other dignitaries, the title of "Rajah" was to be conferred on Tej Singh, Commander-in-Chief of the Lahore army, betwixt whom and the Maharanee Jinda there reigned a bitter enmity. The latter, therefore, delayed her son's arrival at the durbar for upwards of an hour, though all the Sikh Sirdars and English officers were assembled and waiting. When at length he did appear, the Maharajah refused to put out his hand to mark the forehead of the new Rajah on his investiture, and by Colonel Lawrence's orders the ceremony had to be performed by a Sikh priest.

The scene is thus described in a private letter from Lord Hardinge to Sir Frederick Currie.[28]

He resolutely played his part, tucked his little hands behind him, threw himself back in his chair, and one of the priests performed the ceremony. In the evening she (the Maharanee) would not allow the Prince to be dressed to see the fireworks. In short she is breeding him up systematically to thwart the Govt., and the English connection. I am now in confidential correspondence with L., and I see no remedy but to remove her from Lahore.....Sooner or later it must come to this, as he grows older it is our duty as his Guardians to remove him from her evil example.

For this open insult to the Resident and durbar, for which she was known to be responsible, the Maharanee was consequently separated from her son, and removed to Sheikopoora, about twenty-five miles from Lahore (August 19th, 1847).

The constant strain of work at the Lahore Residency was too much for Henry Lawrence's health, and he was obliged to return to England on sick leave, in company with his friend Lord Hardinge, whose period of office had just expired, and who was succeeded as Governor-General, by the Earl of Dalhousie, on the 21st of January, 1848.

Sir Henry Lawrence had left the Punjab, as he believed, in a condition of internal peace; and so little anticipation was generally felt of any serious outbreak in that quarter, that Lord Hardinge had assured his successor, John Lawrence on handing over the reins of government, that, so far as he could see, "it would not be necessary to fire a gun in India for seven years to come!"[29] How speedily was this fair prediction to be falsified, and these bright hopes dashed to the ground!

"The thunder-bolt fell, as it were, out of the blue sky."[30] Towards the end of April, the Punjab was ringing from end to end with the intelligence of the murder of Vans Agnew and Anderson at Multan, and the revolt of Mulraj, the Dewan and Governor of the province, who had raised once more the standard of the Khalsa, calling on all true Sikhs to join him in freeing their country from the rule of the foreigner.

Revolt in Multan

There is no need to tell over again the story of the revolt. Had the military authorities, either at Lahore or Simla, shown only one tithe of the energy displayed by Lieutenant Herbert Edwardes, who, with a single native infantry regiment, 300 horse, and a couple of horse-artillery guns as a nucleus, set about collecting and raising troops, defeated the Dewan in two pitched battles, and finally confined him within the walls of his own city and fortress of Multan, the whole rebellion might have been suppressed as rapidly as it rose, and the necessity for the Second Sikh War have never existed.[31]

Although by the terms of the Treaty of Bhyrowal (see Articles vii., viii., ix.), a British force was specially provided "for the preservation of the peace of the country," for whose services the Lahore Government were annually to pay the sum of twenty-two lakhs of rupees,[32] and although Lord Hardinge had specially arranged for such an emergency, by providing a British movable brigade to be kept always in readiness at Lahore, Sir Frederick Currie hesitated on his own responsibility to order the march of that brigade. Sending instead for the Sikh Sirdars, he told them that they must put down the rebellion and bring the offenders to justice, by their own means, as their only hope of saving their Government. The astonished Sirdars, "after much discussion, declared themselves unable, without British aid, to coerce Dewan Mulraj in Multan, and bring the perpetrators of the outrage to justice."[33]

Some little light is thrown on this seemingly unaccountable action of Sir Frederick Currie, when we recollect that, as Foreign Secretary to the Government of India and as Member of Council, he was doubtless cognizant of many considerations then influencing the new Cabinet at home, but which were unknown to the general public;

26

and we find from a perusal of certain private letters which passed between him and Lord Hardinge,[34] that, as far back as April, 1847, Currie was aware that matters at home pointed more and more "decidedly to eventual annexation of the Punjab."

Believing, therefore, that any serious revolt among the Sikhs, which should necessitate the employment of British arms to suppress it, would only hasten this measure, Currie, in thus sending for the Sirdars, had apparently in his mind, the desire to offer them another chance for the continuance of the native Government, so far as it then existed.

The Sikh Durbar having acknowledged their incapability of coping unaided with the rebellion, Sir Frederick Currie strongly urged on the Governor General and Commander-in-Chief the advisability of the interposition of the British Government, and the immediate despatch of a sufficient force of troops and siege-guns from Ferozepore; but to this Lord Gough would not agree, and the only support given to Edwardes was a force of 5,000 Sikh troops, under Rajah Shere Singh Atareewalah.

Meanwhile, on the 8th May, a plot against the Resident and British officials was discovered at Lahore, in which the Queen-Mother was implicated. Her *vakeel*,[40] Ganga Ram, was one of the chief conspirators, and, together with one Kanh Singh, late a Colonel of Sikh Artillery, was convicted and hanged. On the 15th of May the Maharanee was removed from the fort of Sheikopura by the Resident's orders, and conveyed under escort to Ferozepore on her way to Benares. Here she remained a State prisoner for nearly a year, until removed for greater security to the fortress of Chunar. Not long after her arrival at this last place, however, she, on the 18th of April, 1849, managed to effect her escape in the disguise of *fakeernee*, (female mendicant) and took refuge in Nepal, where she came under the charge of Dr. James Dryburgh Login, who was then Acting-Assistant Resident at Khatmandu.

Order to Remove Maharanee Jinda

The order for the removal of the Maharanee Jinda was signed by three members of the Council of Regency, and by Gulab Singh, on behalf of his absent brother, Rajah Shere Singh Atareewalah. "The venerable Fakeer Nur-ud-deen, personal friend and adviser of the late Maharajah Ranjeet Singh, and a person greatly respected by the Sikhs generally,"[41] personally saw to the order being carried out.

So urgent was Major Edwardes in appealing to Lahore for a few regular regiments, heavy guns, &c., offering with the help of these to close Mulraj's accounts in a fortnight, and obviate the necessity of assembling 50,000 men in October,[42] that Currie, on the 1st July, on his own responsibility, and against the advice of the Commander-in-Chief, ordered the march of the movable brigade under his orders; yet so many delays ensued, owing to want of carriage, and references back and forwards between Simla and Lahore, that it was not until the 24th of the month that the brigade left Lahore under General Whish, and it did not reach Multan till the 18th August—the siege-guns only coming into camp on the 4th of the following month.

On the 14th September the siege was raised, owing to the defection of the Durbar troops under Rajah Shere Singh,[43] and was not resumed until the 26th December, after more than three months and a half of inaction. On the 2nd January 1849 (seven days after the siege was undertaken in earnest), the city was taken by assault; while on the 22nd the citadel was breached, and Mulraj had surrendered unconditionally.

Punjab in Blaze

But by this time the Punjab was in a blaze, and Shere Singh defiant at the head of 30,000 men!

This is not the place to tell over again the history of the Second Sikh War, with its surprising blunderings and bloody victories— victories won at the point of the sword, from an heroic foe driven to desperation, the Sikh Khalsa at bay, and battling for its very existence! Suffice it to say, that on the 18th December Lord Gough crossed the Chenab with his army; that on the 13th January, 1849, with 15,000 men, he fought the battle of Chillianwallah, late in the afternoon, with darkness creeping up, and with troops who had been under arms since early day-break. On the 21st, February, having on the previous day been joined by General Whish's force, set free by the fall of Multan, Lord Gough retrieved all the previous errors of the campaign, by gaining the crowning victory of Gujerat, driving the Sikh army of 34,000 men,

28

totally routed and in confusion, across the Jhelum. On the 14th March, Shere Singh, Chuttur Singh, and the rest of the Sirdars, gave up their swords, and the last remains of the Khalsa army—to the number of 16,000 men—flung down their arms at the summons of General Gilbert, on the upland plains of Rawalpindee.

Thus ended the Second Sikh War, whose origin and motive we must look for in the ranks of that residue of the Khalsa army which, contrary to the advice of the Sikh Commander-in-Chief, we retained as the standing army of the Punjab,[44] while at the same time we took from them the authority and influence they had arrogated to themselves in the government of the country, and reduced the pay and privileges they had been accustomed to fix for themselves at their "own sweet will." Discontented, sullen, and revengeful, they formed a tempting instrument, ready to hand for any turbulent and intriguing spirit, desirous of upsetting the present state of affairs, and involving the Punjab in general confusion for their own advantage.[45]

On this subject Major Edwardes thus wrote to the Resident:[46]

The people of the Punjab repose contentedly under the protection our courts of justice afford them against the great; and our only enemies are the Sikh army whom we spared in 1846.

A proof that the discontent was not universal is seen in the fact that the rebellion spread very slowly. Up to October 4th, no Sirdar had joined Chattur Singh, "who was in despair at the refusals he had received from the Sikh officers at Peshwar." It was not until October, when Mulraj had been six months in rebellion, that the troops at Bunnoo and Peshawar broke into mutiny. The disaffection was throughout mainly confined to the Sikhs, who were dreading the extinction of the Khalsa, and "a large proportion of the inhabitants, especially the Mohammedans," as Lord Dalhousie says in one of his despatches, "took no part in the hostilities, and had no sympathy with the Khalsa army." Even among the Sikhs, who form but one-sixth of the population, there were thirty-four Sirdars, who with their relatives and dependants took no part in the rebellion. Six out of eight members of the Council of Regency remained loyal, and one of these was Bhai Nidhan Singh, called in the official despatches "head of the Sikh religion." Sirdar Khan Singh (whom Vans Agnew was to instal as Dewan in Mulraj's place), and Guldeep Singh, the commandant of the

29

escort, openly defied Mulraj, and were put in irons and most cruelly treated; both died in confinement. Several Sirdars and officers of the Durbar did good service throughout the war, on the British side, notably Sheikh Imam-ud-deen and Misr Sahib Dyal, who co-operated with Lord Gough's army, the latter being attached to the Commander-in-Chief's headquaters as "chief officer on the part of the Durbar;"[47] and the Resident, writing to the Governor-General on the 16th August, assured him that "the conduct of the Durbar, collectively and individually," had been "entirely satisfactory in everything connected with this outbreak, and indeed in all other respects for the last two months."

Whilst the Second Sikh War was in progress, matters remained in *statu quo* at Lahore, the city being perfectly quiet and unaffected by the disturbances in the northern and western provinces. The Resident continued to exercise supreme authority, assisted by the Durbar (except that one member who had gone into open rebellion), and the little Maharajah remained in profound ignorance that any unusual events which could affect him or his sovereignty were passing in the country without.

He knew only that Golab Singh, the son of Chuttur Singh, and his own personal companion, was suddenly removed from his attendance and placed in confinement, and that later on, the palace itself was guarded by a British regiment.[48]

The insurgents were proclaimed as rebels "against the Government of the Maharajah Duleep Singh," and the Resident, on the 18th, November, issued a proclamation (approved by the Governor-General), telling "all loyal subjects to the Maharajah" that the British army "has entered the Lahore territories, not as an enemy to the constituted Government, but to restore order and obedience." It is addressed "to the subjects, servants, and dependents of the Lahore State," and all "who have remained faithful in their obedience to the Government of the Maharajah Duleep Singh....who are not concerned, directly or indirectly, in the present disturbances, are assured that they have nothing to fear from the coming of the British army."[49]

It will serve to give some notion of the contradictory opinions, and confusion of theories, then prevailing in the official world, if we compare this proclamation with a sentence from a despatch of the

30

Secretary to the Government of India, written to the Resident on October 3rd of the same year, i.e., six weeks previously.[50]

> I am desired to intimate to you that the Governor-General in Council considers the State of Lahore to be, to all intents and purposes, directly at war with the British Government, and he expects that those who may be, directly or indirectly, concerned in these proceedings will be treated accordingly by yourself and your officers.

Annexation of Punjab

At length, on the 30th of March, 1849, from the camp at Ferozepore, the Governor-General issued the famous manifesto, which announced that the Government of India was now resolved "on the entire subjection of a people whom their own Government has long been unable to control, and whom no punishment can deter from violence, no acts of friendship conciliate to peace;" and it then became known that Mr. Henry Elliot, the Secretary to the Government of India, had been despatched to Lahore, where he arrived on the 28th of the month, commissioned by Lord Dalhousie to offer terms to the Council of Regency, on the annexation of the country to the British dominions.

Last Treaty of Lahore

LAHORE, *March 29th,* 1849

Terms granted to the Maharajah Duleep Singh Bahadoor, on the part of the Honourable East India Company, by Henry Miers Elliot, Esq., Foreign Secretary to the Government of India, and Lieut-Colonel Sir Henry Montgomery Lawrence, K.C.B., Resident, in virtue of the power vested in them, by the Right Honourable James, Earl of Dalhousie, Knight of the Most Ancient Order of the Thistle, one of Her Majesty's Most Honourable Privy Council, Governor-General, appointed by the Honourable East India Company, to direct and control all their affairs in the East Indies; and accepted, on the part of His Highness the Maharajah, by Rajah Tej Singh, Rajah Deena Nath, Bhai Nidhan Singh, Fakeer Nooruddin, Gundur Singh, agent of Sirdar Shere Singh Sindanwallah, and Sirdar Lal Singh, agent and son of Sirdar Uttur Singh Kaleewallah, members of the Council of Regency, invested with full powers and authority on the part of His Highness.

I.   His Highness the Maharajah Duleep Singh shall resign for himself, his heirs, and his successors all right, title, and claim to the

31

sovereignty of the Punjab, or to any sovereign power whatever.

II.   All the property of the State, of whatever description and wheresoever found, shall be confiscated to the Honourable East India Company, in payment of the debt due by the State of Lahore to the British Government and of the expenses of the war.

III.   The gem called the Koh-i-noor, which was taken from Shah Sooja-ool-moolk by Maharajah Runjeet Singh, shall be surrendered by the Maharajah of Lahore to the Queen of England.

IV.   His Highness Duleep Singh shall receive from the Honourable East India Company, for the support of himself, his relatives, and the servants of the State, a pension of not less than four, and not exceeding five, lakhs of Company's rupees per annum.

V.   His Highness shall be treated with respect and honour. He shall retain the title of Maharajah Duleep Singh Bahadoor, and he shall continue to receive during his life such portion of above-named pension as may be allotted to himself personally, provided he shall remain obedient to the British Government, and shall reside at such place as the Governor-General of India may select.

Granted and accepted at Lahore on the 29th of March, 1849, and ratified by the Right Honourable the Governor-General on the 5th of April, 1849.

(Signed)

DALHOUSIE—MAHARAJAH DULEEP SINGH

H.M.ELLIOT—RAJAH TEJ SINGH

H.M.LAWRENCE—   RAJAH DEENA NATH

                 BHAEE NIDHAN SINGH[51]

                 FAKEER NOORUDDIN

                 GUNDUR SINGH

                 (Agent to SIRDAR SHERE SINGH, SINDANWALLAH)

                 SIRDAR LAL SINGH

                 (Agent and son of SIRDAR UTTUR SINGH, KALEEWALLAH)

Sir Henry Lawrence had by this time returned to his post at Lahore, having hurried out from England in hot haste on receipt of the news of the outbreak at Multan. Landing at Bombay in December, he lost no time in joining the camp of the besiegers—was present at the capture of the city of Multan, and on the 9th of January took the news of that event to the Governor-General. He then joined Lord Gough's headquarters, witnessed the battle of Chillianwallah, and proceeded on the 18th to take up his duties at the Residency.

It would be affectation to conceal the fact, that Lord Dalhousie's views and Sir Henry Lawrence's did not coincide as regards the policy of annexation, and indeed the Governor-General's decision was a sore grief to the generous-hearted Resident, and a reversal of many cherished hopes and projects. Speaking in vindication of this dearly-loved friend of his, in after years, Login says :-

Lawrence acted in the best faith for the interest of both Governments; and so far from desiring the annexation of the country, on finding that it could not be avoided, and that all his efforts to uphold the native Government were unavailing, he was only prevented from resigning his high position, and returning to his regiment as a Captain of Artillery, by the earnest entreaty of his friends. He remained at Lahore with the sole object of exerting his influence to conciliate the chiefs and people of the Punjab to our rule.[52]

When John Lawrence's counsel was sought as to whether the annexation determined on should be carried out now, when the people were depressed by recent defeat, or later, when they had been more perfectly subdued, he gave it without hesitation—"No delay! The Khalsa must not be allowed to raise its head."

His advice was taken, and Mr. Henry Elliot was sent to announce the decision of the Governor-General to the Maharajah and his people.

We will leave Mr. Elliot to tell, in his own words, the manner and purpose of his mission.[53]

Immediately on my arrival, he says, I communicated to Sir H.M. Lawrence and Mr. J. Lawrence the instructions with which I was charged, and regretted to find that both those officers were fully persuaded that the Council of Regency would on no account be induced to accede to the terms which were offered for their acceptance inasmuch as they had already incurred great odium amongst their countrymen for what were considered to be their former concessions. I, however, requested that the two most

33

influential members of the Council might be at once summoned to a private conference at the Residency; and Rajah Tej Singh and Dewan Deena Nath were accordingly sent for. The Rajah, at first, excused himself on the ground of sickness; and I should have, consequently, gone to his house, had I not been apprehensive that any exhibition of undue eagerness might have been interpreted into too great a desire to obtain his concurrence. It was then intimated to him that, as my mission was urgent, and could not be accomplished without him, he should come to the Residency, unless he really was seriously ill. Upon this, he came, his looks giving no warrant for his excuses, and was accompanied by Dewan Deena Nath.

After the first compliments had been exchanged, I explained to them the purpose for which I had come, that the Punjab would be annexed to the British dominions at all events, but that it was for them to decide whether they would subscribe to the conditions which I was about to lay before them.

The Rajah, who was more than usually nervous and garrulous, opened out in a strain of invective against Rajah Shere Singh and all the rebellious Sirdars, who had brought the Council to this pass; acknowledged that the British Government had acquired a perfect right to dispose of the country as it saw fit, and recommended that it should declare its will, without calling upon the Council to sign any conditions. I replied that, if they refused to accept the terms which the Governor-General offered , the Maharajah and themselves would be entirely at his mercy, and I had no authority to say that they would be entitled to receive any allowance whatever.

The Dewan, who was much more deliberate and reserved than his colleague, commented on the severity of the conditions, and particularly on the expatriation of the Maharajah; and when I told him it was intended to exclude also the female relatives of the Maharajah from the palace, in order that the citadel might be exclusively in British occupation, he remarked that, immediately they were relieved from the restraints which their present residence subjected them to, they would begin leading licentious lives, and bring scandal upon the memory of Ranjeet Singh and his descendants.

After many inquiries from them about the distance to which the Maharajah was to be removed, I observed that his destination would not improbably be the Deccan, but, after they had requested reconsideration, on account of the remoteness of that country, "where", said they, "God knows whether the people are Hindus or Mohammedans," I promised that the Maharajah should not be sent anywhere to the east of the Ganges, pointing out Hurdwar, Gurhmuktesir, Bithoor, and Allahabad as being all of them places of high sanctity in their religion. They seemed to be thankful for this as a concession. But they had no definite notion of the exact position of any of these places except Hurdwar. The Rajah, indeed, was astonished to discover that Lahore was not so far from Allahabad as from Benares.

They seemed fully satisfied with the personal allowance assigned to the Maharajah, which I told them would be about 10,000 rupees per mensem.

Other subjects were then discussed, and they enquired anxiously about their own future position. I told them that it was not intended to deprive them of their *jagheers* or salaries, and that, for this indulgence they would be expected to yield the British Government the benefit of their advice and assistance whenever they were called upon to do so; that, if they did not subscribe to the conditions, I could not promise that any consideration would be shown to them. The Dewan enquired whether the *jagheers* would be continued to future generation, I replied, certainly not, unless the grants conveyed a perpetual title ; and that would be left to the decision of the officers, who would shortly be appointed to investigate the validity of all rent -free tenures.

After much more parley, during which, while I told them that they were at perfect liberty to decline, or to accede to, the conditions I had been instructed to lay before them, at the same time I convinced them of my resolute determination to yield no point, they expressed their willingness to sign the paper, and signed it accordingly, not without evident sorrow and repugnance on the part of the Dewan.

Upon this I requested that Fakeer Nurudeen and Bhai Nidhan Singh, the only other members of the Regency resident at Lahore, might be sent for; and upon informing them of what had passed, they said they would abide by whatever their colleagues were prepared to do.

They then affixed their seals and signatures to the paper in duplicate, and Sir H M. Lawrence and myself then added our counter-signatures. It was agreed that next morning a Durbar should be held at seven o' clock, a.m., in order to promulgate the Articles subscribed to, and to obtain the Maharajah's ratification.

The members then took their leave, after the conference had lasted about two hours.

Sir J. Login, commenting on the above report in 1860, remarks:—

"It indicates feelings more creditable to the members of the Lahore Durbar (whose personal interests were separately worked upon) than to the British official, who describes the scene with so much undignified exultation."

To continue Mr. Elliot's report :-

Next day at the appointed hour,[54] after the troops had been prepared against possible tumult, I proceeded to the Durbar, accompanied by Sir H.M. Lawrence, K.C.B. and the gentlemen of the Residency, and escorted by a squadron of the body-guard, which Major Mayne had brought over by forced marches from Ferozepore. We were met by Maharajah Duleep Singh outside the gate of the citadel. After the usual salutations, and giving and taking of presents, we conducted the Maharajah to a seat at the end of the Hall of Audience, and took our places on either side of him . The Maharajah, who is endowed with an intelligence beyond his years, and cannot be supposed to have been ignorant of the purpose for which the Durbar was now convened for the last time, conducted himself throughout with cheerfulness and self-composure.

The hall was filled with spectators, who ranged themselves on each side of the centre seats—the Europeans on the right, the natives on the left. The latter were in such numbers as almost to give cause that, with a view of courting popularity, the Council of Regency might refuse to abide by the terms which they had signed the evening before.

After we were seated, the following note, declaratory of the intentions of the Government to assume the sovereignty of the Punjab, was read out in Persian, and afterwards translated into Hindustani, for the comprehension of every one present:-

MANIFESTO TO THE LAHORE DURBAR

For many years, while the wisdom of Maharajah Ranjeet Singh ruled the people of the Punjab, friendships and unbroken peace prevailed between the British nation and the Sikhs.

The British Government desired to maintain with the heirs of Ranjeet Singh the same friendly relations which they had held with him. But the Sirdars and Sikh army, forgetful of the policy which the Maharajah's prudence had enjoined, and departing from the friendly example he had set, suddenly crossed the frontier, and, without any provocation, made war upon the British power.

They were met by the British army—four times they were defeated—they were driven back with ignominy across the Sutlej, and pursued to the walls of Lahore.

The Maharajah Duleep Singh tendered there, to the Governor-General of India, the submission of himself and his chiefs, and implored the clemency of the British Government.

The Government of India had acquired, by its conquest, an absolute right to subvert the Government of the Sikhs, by which it had been so grossly injured. But in that time of victory, it showed the sincerity of its declarations, and gave signal proof of the moderation and forbearance by which its policy was directed.

The kingdom of the Punjab was spared; the Maharajah was replaced on the throne of Ranjeet Singh; and treaties of friendship were formed between the States.

How have the obligations of these treaties been fulfilled?

The British Government has, with scrupulous fidelity, observed every promise which was made, and has discharged every obligation which the treaties imposed upon it.

It gave to the Maharajah the service of its troops. It afforded him the aid of its treasures in his difficulties. It meddled with none of the institutions or customs of the people. By its advice to the Council it improved the condition of the army; and it laboured to lessen the burdens and to promote the prosperity of every class of the Maharajah's people. It left nothing undone which it had promised to perform; it engaged in nothing from which it had promised to abstain. But there is not one of the main provisions of those treaties which the Sikh Government and Sikh people have not, on their part, faithlessly and flagrantly violated. They bound themselves to pay an annual subsidy of twenty-two lakhs of rupees. No portion whatever has at any time been paid.

36

The whole debt due by the State of Lahore has increased to more than fifty lakhs of rupees; and crores have been added by the charges of the present war. The control of the British Government, which the Sirdars themselves invited, and to which they bound themselves to submit, has been rejected and resisted by force.

The peace and friendship which were promised by the treaties have been thrown aside. British officers in the discharge of their duty have treacherously been thrown into captivity, with women and children.

Other British officers, when acting for the Maharajah's interests, were murdered by the Maharajah's servants, after having been deserted by the Maharajah's troops.

Yet, for these things, the Government of Lahore neither inflicted punishment on the offender, nor made reparation for the offence. It confessed itself unable to control its subjects. It formally declared to the British Resident that its troops would not obey its command, and would not act against the chief who had committed this outrage against the Government of India.

Not only did the army of the State refuse thus to act, but it everywhere openly rose in arms against the British. The whole people of the Sikhs joined in its hostility. The high Sirdars of the State have been its leaders; those of them who signed the treaties of peace were the most conspicuous in its ranks; and the chief by whom it was commanded was a member of the Council of Regency itself. They proclaimed their purpose to be the extirpation of the British power, and the destruction of the British people; and they have struggled fiercely to effect it.

But the Government of India has put forth the vast resources of its power. The Army of the Sikhs has been utterly discomfited; their artillery has been captured, the allies they invited have been driven from the Punjab with shame; the Sikh Sirdars, with their troops, have surrendered, and been disarmed, and the Punjab is occupied by the British troops.

The Government of India repeatedly declared that it desired no further conquest; and it gave to the Maharajah, by its acts, a proof of the sincerity of its declarations.

The Government of India has sought and desires no conquest now.

But when unprovoked and costly war has again been wantonly renewed, the Government of India is bound by its duty to provide for its own security for the future, and to guard effectually the interests and tranquillity of its own people.

Punishment and benefit alike have failed to remove the inveterate hostility of the Sikhs. Wherefore, the Governor-General, as the only effectual mode which now remains of preventing the recurrence of national outrage, and the renewal of perpetual wars, has resolved upon declaring the British Sovereignty in the Punjab, and upon the entire subjection of the Sikh nation, whom their own rulers have long been unable to control, who are equally insensible to punishment or forbearance, and who, as past events have now shown, will never desist from war so long as they possess the power of an independent kingdom.

The Governor-General of India unfeignedly regrets that he should feel himself

37

compelled to depose from his throne a descendant of Maharajah Ranjeet Singh, while he is yet in his early youth.

But the Sovereign of every State is responsible for, and must be affected by, the acts of his people over whom he reigns.

As in the former war, the Maharajah, because of the lawless violence of his subjects, whom his Government was unable to control, was made to pay the penalty of their offence in the loss of his richest provinces; so must he now be involved in all the consequences of their further violence, and of the deep national injury they again have committed.

When a renewal of formidable war by the army and the great body of Sikhs has forced upon the Government of India the conviction that a continuance of Sikh domination in the Punjab is incompatible with the security of the British Territories, the Governor-General cannot permit that mere compassion for the Prince should deter him from the adoption of such measures against the nation as alone can be effectual for the future maintenance of peace, and for protecting the interests of the British people.

Upon the conclusion of this Manifesto, silence was observed for a few minutes, when Dewan Deena Nath observed, that the decision of the British Government was just, and should be obeyed; but he trusted that the Maharajah and the servants of the State would receive consideration at the hands of the British Government, and that some allowance would be granted to maintain them in comfort and respectability.

"If France," he observed, "after the defeat and captivity of Buonaparte, had been restored to its legitimate ruler, though the country yielded thirty crores of revenue, it would be no very extraordinary act of British clemency if the Punjab, which yielded less than three crores, should be restored to the Maharajah. However, let the Governor-General's will be done."

I replied, that the time of concession and clemency was gone; that I was ready, on the part of the Governor-General, to confirm the conditions to which the Council had subscribed yesterday, and which should be read out in Persian and Hindustani, for general information.

This was listened to with the deepest attention, but it called forth no observation. To the former signatures were then added those of Gundur Singh, the accredited Agent of Sirdar Shere Singh, Sindunwallah, and Sirdar Lal Singh, Agent and son of Sirdar Uttur Singh, Kaleewallah, thus completing the entire number of the members of the Council of Regency, who have remained nominally faithful to their engagements. The paper was then handed in duplicate by Rajah Tej Singh to the Maharajah, who immidiately affixed his signature, by tracing the initials of his name in English letters. The alacrity with which he took the papers when offered to him, was a matter of remark to all, and suggested the idea that, possibly, he had been instructed by his advisers that any show of hesitation might lead to the substitution of terms less favourable than those which had been offered.

When the document had thus been fully ratified, I directed the proclamation to be read aloud in the native languages.

I then handed one copy of the terms to the Maharajah; and having thus fulfilled the object of my mission, I took my leave with the usual etiquette, and dissolved the Durbar.

The whole ceremony was conducted with grave decorum. No Sirdar was armed. The costly jewels and gaudy robes, so conspicuous in the Sikh court on other public occasions, were now thrown aside. I did not observe the slightest sign of wonder, sorrow, anger, or even dissatisfaction, upon the countenance of any one present, except that of Dewan Deena Nath; and from the nice inquiries he had made during the private conference, respecting his own interests, it would not be uncharitable to suppose, that his sadness arose more from the loss of the immense influence he possesses in every department of the State, than from regret at the subversion of his master's dynasty. But neither did I observe any signs of gladness. The whole announcement appeared to be received with a degree of indifference bordering on apathy, and not a word or whisper escaped, to betray the real feelings pervading the hearts of that solemn assembly, which had met to witness the ratified dissolution of the great empire established by the fraud and violence of Ranjeet Singh.

As I left the palace, I had the proud satisfaction of seeing the British colours hoisted on the citadel under a royal salute from our own artillery, at once proclaiming the ascendancy of British rule, and sounding the knell of the Khalsa Raj!

"That the annexation of the Punjab was a politic measure," says Sir John Login,[55] " few were inclined to question, but, *inasmuch as it involved the deposition of a young Prince whom the British Government had solemnly engaged to protect in his position during his minority, and who had throughout evinced the utmost confidence in us*, it was, to say the least, a harsh proceeding, and one which demanded from our Government towards the person whom our policy despoiled, the most liberal and generous consideration.

"Unfortunately, however, in the Maharajah's case, there were circumstances which had the effect of placing the position of His Highness in unfavourable contrast to that of his ministers and chiefs, and which, unless obviated in a liberal spirit, necessarily led to the conclusion, that, in accepting the terms offered by the British Government, his ministers had consented to *sacrifice his interests to their own*.

Maharajah Declared State Property

"Having, so far as respects their claims upon him, been considered by the British Government, notwithstanding the full control exercised by their officials over his person, power, and resources, to be in the position of a Sovereign and despotic Prince, every article of property in the possession of the Maharajah was declared to be State property, and appropriated by the British Government, under the terms which had been granted to him; His Highness being merely permitted to retain, by the courtesy of the Governor-General and the local authorities, such articles as were considered necessary for his personal use.

"He was thus made entirely dependent upon the allowance assigned to him, under Aricle v., by the British Government, amounting during his minority to £12,000 per annum; another portion of the State pension being granted to his relatives and dependents, at the discretion of the British Government, and a balance retained by them for future appropriation

"No stipulation was made for the benefit of his heirs and decendants, the pension granted to him being apparently terminable with his life. He was required to remove from the Punjab, and from all his early associations, and to reside wherever the Government of India might appoint.

"To His Highness' ministers, Sirdars, and chiefs, the annexation of the Punjab was attended with more favourable circumstances.

"They were relieved from the claims of a Native Government, as feudatories of a despotic Prince, liable to contributions for state purposes—secured in all their private property, real and personal, under British Laws—confirmed in possession of their several *jagheers*, some in perpetuity, others rent-free for their own lives, and with deductions of one-half and one-quarter in two succeeding generations; and they were exempted from much personal service to their Prince.

"Having seen that, in 1846, Gulab Singh, one of their number, was not only made independent of Lahore, but was allowed to purchase the Province of Kashmir, the chiefs who remained faithful were naturally not indisposed to enter into terms with a Government which could act so liberally, and relieve them from demands frequently made by their princes.

"To Rajah Tej Singh in particular the arrangement must have been very satisfactory, as it secured to him and his heirs all his accumulations (amounting in 1846, as shown by his offer for an independent territory like Gulab Singh, to not less than twenty-five lakhs of rupees), confirming him and his family for three generations in large estates, very lightly assessed, it is believed, at two and three lakhs of rupees; and yearly increasing in value.

"In the same manner, the other chiefs had more or less cause to be satisfied. Even those who had been in arms against us, though deprived of such property *as could not be concealed,* were doubtless able to secure very large sums among their friends. In the case of Rajah Shere Singh, the writer of this was told, by himself, that such was the case, when he wished to obtain permission to go to England, instead of being sent to Calcutta.

"It was not considered expedient at the time to be too particular, and I think it will be found, on reference to Treasury receipts from forfeited estates, that very little was obtained, compared with the wealth of which, a short time before, the chiefs were known to have been in possession.

"This leniency has not been without its good effects, and the security with which Sikh chiefs have been allowed to enjoy their wealth, without exaction from Government, has no doubt contributed greatly to reconcile them to our rule.

"But it must not be overlooked, that all this liberality was shown at the expense of the claims of their Sovereign Prince, on both feudatories and rebels."

"[56]Although the young Maharajah could not but feel that the terms which had been imposed on him were hard and severe, especially when the loss of his throne was occasioned by no fault on his part, but *entirely* from the treachery of those whom we had placed in power around him, the difficulties with which he had been surrounded in his precarious position, before he was received under the protection of the British Government, were too strongly impressed on his mind to cause any hesitation on his part to retire into private life, and he accordingly submitted to the force of circumstances with very becoming dignity."

References

1. From *panch,* "five;" ab, "water."

2. The total population of the Punjab, in 1881, including the Native States, was 22,712,120. Exclusive of the Native States, it is 18,850,437.

3. Cunningham's *"History of the Sikhs,"* p. 2.

4. Gross receipt's for the year ending March 31st, 1884—£4,810,825.

5. Govind assumed the Guruship in 1695.

6. The word *Khalsa* signifies "pure, special, free." According to the teaching of Govind, every Sikh, as such, was equally a member of the Khalsa, which was regarded as the depository of Divine authority upon earth, and in whose collective body God Himself was held to be mystically present.

7. The essentials for this were : 1st. The presence of five Sikhs (disciples). "Where five Sikhs were assembled," says Govind, "there is the Khalsa." 2nd. Some sugar and water stirred together in a vessel with a two-edged dagger or other iron weapon. The candidate repeats the articles of his faith , a portion of the water is sprinkled over him, and he drinks the remainder with the exclaimation, "Hail Guru!" See Cunningham, *Note,* p. 76.

8. Prinsep's *"History of the Sikhs,"* p. 28. The principal Misls were twelve in number, viz :- 1. Bhungee. 2. Kuneia or Ghunneya. 3. Sooker-Chukea. 4. Ramgurhea. 5. Phoolkea. 6. Nukeia. 7. Allowalea. 8. Duleeals. 9. Nishanwalea. 10. Krorea Singhea. 11. Shudeed and Nihang. 12. Fyzool Lapoorea or Singhpoorea.

9. Prinsep, p. 39.

10. *Memorandum drawn up for Her Majesty* by Sir John Login. See also Cunningham, p. 186.

11. Rajah Gulab Singh (made afterwards Maharajah of Kashmir by the English), Dhyan Singh and Suchet Singh, three brothers, who were powerful favourites of Ranjeet Singh.

12. See Cunningham, p. 244; also Symth's *"Reigning Family of Lahore";* Steinbach. Henry Lawrence's *"Adventurer in the Punjab,"* &c.

13. Descendants of Nodha, an ancestor of Ranjeet Singh.

14. Symth's *"Reigning Family of Lahore,"* p. 76.

15. Cunningham, p. 271. Shere Singh had left a son (Sheo Deo Singh), then an infant of four months, and also three adopted sons,—*Memo. by Sir J. Login.*

16. Cunningham, p. 278.

17. Afterwards created Viscount Hardinge.

18. *"Life of Lord Lawerence,"* vol. i., p. 191.

19. *"Maharajah Duleep Singh and the Government,"* p. 71. See also *"Life of Sir Herberts Edwardes,"* vol. i., p. 44.

20. The war had cost the victors dearly in men and officers. Among fifty-six of the latter, who fell in the bloody fight of Ferozepore, was the noble-hearted D'Arcy Todd, Login's late chief at Herat, to whom he was attached by the closest bonds of intimacy and affection.

21. See *"Treaty of Bhyrowal."* Appendix.

22. Quoted from *"Maharajah Duleep Singh,"* p. 30.

23. *"Punjab Papers,"* 1849, pp. 35,48,53.

24. *"Punjab Papers,"* 1849, p. 18.

25. Dated October 23rd, 1847.

26. *"Life of Sir Henry Lawrence,* K. C. B.," vol. ii., p. 100.

27. "Punjab Papers,"1849, p. 32.

28. Dated August 19th, 1847. Private Papers of the Late Sir F. Currie (by kind permission of Lady Currie.)

29. *"Life of Lord Lawrence,"* by Bosworth Smith, vol. i., p. 245.

30. *"India under Victoria,"* by Captain Trotter, vol. i., p.171

31. Alone, unsupported, he (Edwardes) achieved a result of which a British army might have been proud. And it is not too much to affirm, that had he been then there supported by a few British troops and guns, placed under his own orders, he might have taken the fortress, and possibly have nipped the rising in the bud.—Malleson's *"Decisive Battles,"* pp. 351, 352.

32. If this sum was *not* paid annually into the Calcutta Treasury, the matter was entirely in the hands of the British Resident, who had supreme control over the revenues and finances of the Punjab. See Articles ii, and vi. of the Treaty of Bhyrowal.—Appendix.

33. *"Punjab Papers,"* 1849, p. 140.

34. *Unpublished Correspondence of Sir Fredrick Currie.*

40. Ambassador, or accredited agent.

41. *"Punjab Papers,"* 1849, p. 169. On her removal to Sheikopoora the Ranee's stipend had been reduced to 48,000 rupees (£4,800); on her banishment to Banaras it was made 12,000 rupees (£1,200).

42. *"Punjab Papers,"* p. 223. I am one of those who believe to this day, perhaps ever shall, that had that brigade, under a fine soldier like Brigadier Campbell, marched AT ONCE upon Mooltan (say on April 25th) the rebellion would have been nipped in the bud by the escape and surrender of Moolraj. . . . Moolraj did not quit because the Sikhs were ready to back him up. The Sikhs backed up Moolraj because the British Government did not put him down. . . . The Sikh insurrection was created out of the materials collected to put the Mooltan rebellion.—Remarks of Sir Herbert Edwards (see his *"Life,"* by Lady Edwardes, 1886, viz. i., p. 145, 147).

43

43. When Currie consulted the Sirdars, they warned him then that these troops were disaffected, and not to be depended on.—*"Punjab Papers,"* p 140.

44. "Rajah Tej Singh said, *two years ago,* and has always adhered to the opinion , that it was less dangerous, and would prove less embarrasing, to disband them all had raise a new army, than to continue a man to them in service."— *Sir F. Currie to Government,* September, 1848.

45. June 22nd the Resident wrote :—The Sirdars are true, I believe; the soldiers are all false, I know.—*"Punjab Papers,"* p. 220.

46. August 27th, 1848. *Unpublished Correspondence of Sir F. Currie.*

47. *"Punjab Papers,"* p. 444. These Sikhs forces are said to have numbered 20,000.—*"Maharajah Duleep Singh and the Government."*

48. This was in consequence of information received from Mooltan. "Look well," says Major Edwardes, writing on the 29th August to the Resident, *"to the person of the Maharajah,* for Shum Shere Singh says, Chuttur Singh will try to get him carried off while out riding, or at the Shalamar Gardens, and then *ask us to account for fighting against Duleep Singh, with whom we made a Treaty!"*—*Unpublished Correspondence of the late Sir F. Currie.*

49. *"Punjab Papers,"* pp. 260, 438, 449, 562.

50. Ibid, p. 374.

51. Head of the Sikh religion.

52. Ferrier's *"Caravan Journey."*—Note by J. S. L., p. 359.

53. Note and Report by Mr. H. Elliot.

54. Report by Mr. Elliot, March 29th, 1849.

55. *Memorandum* published (for private circulation) in 1860.

56. *Memorandum prepared for Her Majesty* by Sir John Login.

DULEEP SINGH AND THE BRITISH GOVERNMENT
1856—1886

With the death of Sir John Login all business communication with the Maharajah ceased, and although a lively interest was taken in his proceedings, by the family which he had hitherto held in such close friendship, it will easily be understood, now that the head and guiding hand had gone from among them, that a gradual drifting apart set in, and much went on in the life of the Maharajah that was unknown to his former friends.

It should be sufficient to give a short summary of the situation of the Maharajah with regard to the Government, and such facts as can be produced from official and other sources will be brought to show how brooding over fancied wrongs, and constant beating against the rocks of cold officialdom, has gone far towards turning a loyal and loving subject of Her Majesty, the first convert to Christanity among the princes of India, into a bitter and discontented foe! His early training led him to trust his guardian (the British Government) implicitly. How has that guardian treated him?

Pecuaniary Claims & Disappointment

To answer this query, let us turn to the evidence of Sir John Login in his private letter to Sir Charles Wood, and the memorandum subsequently drawn up by him on the Maharajah's position with the Government:-

July, 1859.

DEAR SIR CHARLES WOOD,

I hope that you will kindly excuse the liberty I take, in intruding upon your attention while it must be so fully occupied with matters of perhaps more importance; but as I am very apprehensive that if I delay to do so an opportunity may be lost of doing an act of justice in a graceful way, and in a manner which may tend to advance the public interests in India very materially, I venture to bring it to your notice.

I have already mentioned to you that the subject of the Maharajah Duleep Singh's settlements on coming of age has been under the consideration of Government since December, 1856, when he became entitled (at eighteen), by the laws of India, to the management of his own affairs, but that various circumstances have prevented a final decision upon the subject up to the present time. He has, during the last three years, been unsettled and anxious regarding it, and to provide against some of the inconveniences likely to arise from the delay, he has been induced to insure his life at an annual premium of £1,000.

With every desire, however, to make allowances for the delay, it is very difficult for a young man at his age to be patient under it, especially when he has already had to pay £3,000 as insurance premium, which would not have been necessary had his settlement been determined at the proper time; and I am therefore apprehensive that if all arrangements are not satisfactorily completed before he attains his majority (on the 4th September, little more than a month hence), he may naturally be very greatly disappointed, and be much less disposed to be satisfied with any settlement which may be made by Government than he now is.

When all the circumstances of the Maharajah's removal from the throne of the Punjab and the annexation of his country are duly considered, I think that it must be admitted to be at least very satisfactory to us, that the person who, in the opinion of other civilized nations, has suffered most from the change should himself, on attaining an age at which he can correctly judge of the rectitude of our proceedings towards him, be ready to express his approbation; and I may be excused, therefore, if I am a little anxious, for the sake of our own high character among other nations, and among the people of India, that nothing should occur to deprive us of this satisfaction.

It has been said, and, perhaps, truely, that the Maharajah has been fortunate in having been removed from his high position into private life at his early age, and also that he could never have continued to hold it, even with the assistance to which he was entitled from us, among so turbulent a people. But even admitting the latter to be the case—although I greatly doubt it—have we not, as a Government, been equally fortunate in having to act with a young man who, during the last ten years, has given us the most convincing proofs of his loyalty, fidelity, and good will, rather than with one who might have been otherwise disposed towards us, and have set a different example to his former subjects?

I have no doubt that you will take these circumstances into consideration in determining the provision to be made for himself and his family, and that notwithstanding the *temporary* difficulties in which the general finances of India are now involved, you will kindly bear in mind that, in so far as respects the Punjab, the result of our Government has been eminently successful, and has far exceeded the anticipations which were formed when, in 1849, the Maharajah was deprived of his throne, and required, through the ministers that we had placed around him, to accept such terms as we imposed upon him.

I confess that I am less anxious for the Maharajah's personal interest in the decision of the question, than for the honour and credit of the British Government, and for the character which impartial history may yet attach to the transaction.

While admitting the necessity of the measure, it was considered at the time by almost all who took part in it to be a very hard proceeding towards the Maharajah, and one which can in no way be so satisfactorily justified, as by his own approval of it, after his judgement has been matured by ten years' experiences, and he has been able to appreciate the motives from which we acted.

Trusting you will excuse the freedom with which I have addressed you.

I remain &c.,

J.S. LOGIN.

MEMORANDUM BY SIR JOHN LOGIN
Written in 1862

Dec. 9th, 1856. The Maharajah wrote to the Court of Directors requesting that his settlement, on coming of age might be taken into consideration.

Feb. 19th, 1857. He was informed, in reply, that a reference would be made to India on the subject. They also released him from the restrictions imposed on him by treaty as to residence.

In consequence of the mutiny of the Bengal Army, and other causes, no further communication was made in this matter until—

May 20th, 1859.— When His Highness was informed by Lord Stanley that Her Majesty's Government proposed to fix his allowance at an annual rate of £25,000, to commence on the attainment of his majority, according to the laws of England.

June 3rd, 1859. The Maharajah acknowledged the liberality of this allowance, but requested to be informed whether it was to be considered a mere annuity for his life, or to be continued in whole or in part to his heirs and descendants.

Oct. 24th, 1859. He was informed by Sir Charles Wood that, of the yearly allowance of £25,000, the sum of £15,000 was to be considered as a personal allowance, terminable with His Highness's life, and the remaining £10,000 to be derived from investment (in

47

the name of trustees) of such an amount of India stock as will yield that amount of yearly interest—such Capital Stock (subject to provisions for his widow, not exceeding £3,000 per annum), to be at His Highness's disposal to bequeath to the legitimate heirs of his body according to the laws of England.

In the event of his leaving no such heirs, the stock to revert to the Government, subject to such settlement as His Highness may have made upon his wife. This arrangement to be in satisfaction of all claims for himself, or his heirs, on the British Government.

Nov. 1st, 1859. The Maharajah expressed his satisfaction at the manner in which it is proposed to make provision for his family—but believing that no inconsiderable portion of the sum which Her Majesty's Government proposed to place in trust for himself and his family had already accumulated by lapses and short payments, during his minority, from the State pension assigned under treaty, he requested that the condition requiring the reversion of the trust fund to Government on failure of direct heirs should be so far modified as to admit of his appropriating such portion of it as can be shown to have accrued up to the period of his decease by accumulations, by lapses, and otherwise, from the State pensions above alluded to, for the promotion of Christian education in the Punjab, or other territories over which he had held sovereignty, placing the same under such additional trustees as may be approved by Her Majesty's Government. He also pointed out that no allusion had been made to his claim for compensation for loss of property during the Mutiny.

No reply having been received to this communication for upwards of two months, the question having, it is believed, been referred to a Special Committee of the Indian Council, and objections, it is said, having been raised to the Maharajah's request, on the grounds of interference with religious neutrality, the Maharajah called Sir Charles Wood at the India Office, and at a private interview stated his claims more fully.

Having been requested by Sir Charles Wood to give in a written document, to be laid before the Council, the following was at once prepared in his presence, and signed by the Maharajah:—

The Maharajah asks for £25,000 a year for life, and also the sum of

48

£200,000 to be settled on him for life, and on his heirs after him; and in the event of no heirs, he is at liberty to devise it for any public purpose in India.

This to be in full of all demands.

Duleep Singh.

Jan. 20th, 1860.

The question having been thus modified by the document which the Maharajah had, without sufficient consideration of his position under the Treaty, given in, and which Sir Charles Wood had also unfortunately overlooked, the Committee of Council had little difficulty in pointing out that the Maharajah had personally no right to any further portion of the State pension than that which had been, or might be, assigned to him by the British Government; and a communication was made to His Highness to this effect.

It was admitted, however, in Sir Charles Wood's letter—that the whole of the State pension fixed by the Government for the Maharajah, his relatives, and servants of the State, had not been expended in each year for the above purpose—that he had no means of ascertaining the whole amount of accumulations arising from this source, but that it may probably be between £150,000 and £200,000—" that Her Majesty's Government have no intention of allowing any part of this amount to be applied to any purposes other than that for which it was assigned."

Sir Charles Wood further stated, that it will rest with the Government of India to determine, how the accumulations ought to be disposed of for the benefit of all parties interested—that he was very decidedly of opinion that the advantage accorded to His Highness, by the capitalizing of a sum yielding £10,000 a year, was greatly in excess of what he could derive from any apportionment of the present accumulation.

If, however, His Highness should be of a different opinion, Sir Charles Wood was ready to call on the Government of India to report the exact amount of the accumulation, and the proportion which could be assigned to His Highness, with due regard to the claims and circumstances of the other parties interested; such amount, in that case, to be at His Highness's absolute disposal,

49

leaving him to make his own arrangements for a provision for his wife and children.

April 3rd, 1860. The Maharajah, in reply to the above letter, explained the circumstances under which he had asked permission to appropriate the trust fund to Christian education in the event of the failure of heirs; expressed his regret at the inadvertence of which he had been guilty in respect to the document which he had given in, at his private interview with Sir Charles Wood, and with reference to Sir Charles Wood's admission as to the state of the account, and that he had no means of ascertaining the actual amount of accumulations from the State pension, repeated a request that he had made in his letter of June 3rd, 1859, to be furnished with a full statement of accounts before he could enter upon any compromise of his claims.

April 20th, 1860. Sir Charles Wood explained a portion of his letter of 23rd march, which His Highness had apparently misunderstood, and stated, that he gathered from His Highness's letter of the 3rd April that His Highness wished to defer his decision between the two alternatives there referred to, until he shall have learned what the sum to be placed at his disposal may be.

April 30th, 1860. His Highness in reply, repeated his wish to decline any compromise or decision, until he had been favoured with the required statement, when he would be prepared to enter into such arrangement as, under the circumstances of his position, may appear expedient.

A further delay of nearly fifteen months having occurred in procuring the required information from India, on—

July 27th, 1861,—His Highness was at length furnished with a copy of the statement, accompanied by a letter from Sir Charles Wood, in which he pointed out that the unappropriated balance of the Lahore State Pension Fund amounted to about £76,500 on the 4th of September, 1859.

INDIA OFFICE, *July 27th,* 1861.

MAHARAJAH.

It appears from the statement, which is made up to the 4th September. 1859

50

(a copy of which is appended to this letter), when your Highness attained your majority, that the total amount appropriated, in accordance with the terms of 1849, falls short of the aggregate sum payable to the Lahore family —viz, four lakhs of rupees per annum—by 764,263 rupees, or about £76,500.

The amount now annually paid to the family is about four and a half lakhs of rupees.

I trust that your Highness will now be able to return without further delay a definite answer to the proposal contained in my letters of 24th October, 1859, and 23rd March, 1860. With reference to these letters, I have only to add that if your Highness should elect to receive the unappropriated balance—say £76,500— I am willing, in accordance with the recommendation of the Government of India, to place the entire amount at the disposal of your Highness, instead of capitalizing a part of your present allowance (that is, £10,000 per annum), for the purposes and in the manner stated in the above-cited letters.

I have the honour to be, &c.,

CHARLES WOOD.

Some of the documents having been omitted to be sent on from the India Office, they were furnished on application.

On referring to the statement forwarded to His Highness, so manifest a discrepancy was at once apparent in the amount to be credited, and in other parts of the account, that, without going into details, it was necessary to ask for explanations, which His Highness accordingly did, in a letter addressed to Sir Charles Wood on the subject.

To SIR CHARLES WOOD

August, 1861.

SIR,

I have had the honour to receive your letter of the 10th instant, with it enclosures, showing the manner in which the balance of £76,500, referred to in your letter of the 27th ult.,has been obtained.

Before entering into the question of the amount to be credited by the Government of India, under Art. 4 of the Treaty of Lahore, of date March 29th, 1849, or into details of disbursements on account of myself, my relatives, and dependants, which had been furnished to me, it is necessary that I should point out that even at the rate assumed by the Government in the abstract which I have now received (viz, four lakhs of rupees per annum), the amount to be credited to the Lahore Pension Fund between 29th March, 1849, and the 4th September, 1859, i.e., for 10 years 5 months and 6 days, would be Company's Rs. 4,173,333. 7.5., exclusive of interest, and not Company's Rs. 4,071,111. 1. 9, as exhibited in the statement.

I would also bring to your notice, that I have not yet been furnished with any statement in detail of the payments made from the General Treasury, amounting, as shown in the abstract, to Company's Rs. 186,000, nor of advances on account of my personal stipend from March, 1855, to the 4th September, 1859, stated to amount to Company's Rs. 475,333, which are necessary to elucidate the account.

With respect to the remarks in the second paragraph of your letter of the 27th ult., that the amount now annually paid is about four lakhs of rupees, I can find nothing in the statement or letters to exhibit this, and I shall therefore be obliged by further information on the subjects.

I have &c.,&c.,

DULEEP SINGH

It had always been the wish and intention of the Maharajah and those who advised him, after being furnished with a statement of the accounts, to place the matter in the hands of impartial persons best qualified to judge of the circumstances of the case, and to abide by their decision, and accordingly, when several months elapsed without any reply to the inquiry for explantion, it was urged upon Sir Charles Wood to refer the question to Sir John Lawrence for settlement, as the person, above all others, best qualified to judge of the circumstances attending the negotiation of the Treaty, and in fact, the officer through whose influence and exertions the Treaty had been obtained. After some delay Sir John Lawrence undertook to act, if assisted by Sir Frederick Currie; and Sir Charles Wood, having made this arrangement, requested the Maharajah to send in a "statement of his wishes and objections" to those two gentlemen, to be submitted by some person duly authorized by him to place the case before them.

His Highness declined sending in any statement, but requested Sir John Login to wait upon Sir John Lawrence and Sir Frederick Currie at the time appointed, to offer any explanations which these gentlemen might require, and expressed his readiness to be perfectly satisfied with any decision which Sir John Lawrence and Sir John Frederick Currie might arrive at on the question, placing his case entirely and unreservedly in their hands.

These gentlemen having accordingly considered the whole question, prepared a report (as a Sub-Committee of Council) for submission to the Secretary of State, but in consequence, it is believed, of some difference of opinion in the Council on the subject, no steps appear to have been taken by Sir Charles Wood to consider their report for nearly three months—when His Highness, becoming impatient at the delay, and being anxious that his mother (then residing with him) should return to India, and that he should accompany her for a short time, applied for, and obtained, permission from Sir Charles Wood for the purpose.

Within a short time, however, after His Highness's wish was intimated to Sir Charles wood, and his consent obtained, the following letter was sent to His Highness from the India Office, under date *July 26th*, 1862:—

Maharajah,

With reference to our first correspondence, I have now the honour to inform your Highness that since the date of my last letter, I have taken into my deliberate consideration in Council, the several accounts which have been laid before me, representing the sums which have been hitherto appropriated to the benefit of your Highness, your relatives, and the servants of the Lahore State, in accordance with the terms of 1849, and I have the satisfaction of adding, that Her Majesty's Government are now prepared to make an arrangement for the future maintenance of yourself and your immediate family, which, it is confidently hoped, will be acceptable to your Highness.

It is proposed that, without reference to your present life pension of £25,000 per annum, which will be maintained on its present footing, the sum of £105,000 (one hundred and five thousand pounds) shall be invested in the purchase of an estate in this country, to be held by trustees for your Highness's benefit, the rent thereof be enjoyed by you in addition to your present stipend. Should your Highness marry, any provision for your widow will be settled upon this estate.

In the event of your leaving lawful issue, you will be empowered to devise the estate to such issue in any proportion that you may think fit, or should you die intestate, the estate will, in such case, pass by inheritance to your children.

Should you have no issue, you would be empowered to devise the estate to such person or persons as you might desire to bestow it upon.

Her Majesty's Government do not, however, mean to limit to the proceeds of the estate, the amount of provision to be made after your death for such legitimate offspring as you may leave behind. They are willing to enable you to devise to such offspring, in such proportions as you may think fit, an amount of four per cent. India Capital Stock as will yield an income of £7,000 per annum and should your Highness die intestate, the Capital Stock above mentioned will

53

pass by inheritance to your legitimate children, according to the laws of this country.

Your Highness will understand, that in making this arrangement for the future provision of yourself and your family—which is irrespective of any arrangement that has been and may hereafter be made, for other objects embraced in the terms of the Treaty of Lahore—Her Majesty's Government intend it to be final, and in satisfaction of all personal claims which you may have upon the British Government, and an acknowledgement to this effect will be required from your Highness, on your acceptance of the present proposal.

Hoping that your Highness will consider this as a satisfactory solution of the question so long pending between you and the British Government, and that you will accept it with the kindly feeling and in the liberal spirit in which it is offered.

I have the honour, &c.,

Charles Wood.

Reply from the Maharajah, *Oct. 11th*, 1862

Sir,

I have the honour to acknowledge the receipt of your letter of 26th July, informing me of the arrangements which Her Majesty's Government are now prepared to make for my future maintenance, and that of my immediate family, and which you confidently hope will be acceptable to me.

In reply, I desire to express my sincere thanks for the careful and deliberate consideration which you have given in council to my personal right as a pensioner under the Treaty of Lahore, and for the kindly feeling which is manifested in the arrangements which are proposed for my benefit and that of my immediate family.

While I regret that the whole question of my claims has not been settled, as I had hoped would have been done when it was referred to Sir John Lawrence and Sir Frederick Currie, I readily accept these arrangements under the conditions which you specify, and I am prepared to sign any legal document which may be necessary to release the Government from any further pecuniary claims on my own part, or that of immediate family, arising out of the Treaty.

But I hope you will agree with me, that in my position under the Treaty, and as head of my family, it is still incumbent upon me to see that fit and proper arrangements should be made for placing the control of the remainder of the State pension under trust, in such manner as may appear most advisable; and I shall be happy to enter into any further arrangements for that purpose that may be requisite.

Your letter does not allude to my claims for compensation for loss of property at Fattehghur during the Mutiny, nor to the appropriation of intestate estates of deceased relatives and members of my family; but these matters I leave confidently in your hands, believing that they will be settled in the same friendly spirit in which the arrangements now proposed have been made.

I have, &c.,

DULEEP SINGH

To the above letter no reply has yet (December 6th, 1862) been received; but it is believed that the Government intend to act upon it by making over the money to be assigned under trust for the Maharajah's own family as proposed.

Now, from the letter to Sir Charles Wood, and from the contentions brought forward in the above memorandum, it will be seen that Sir John Login himself did not consider that the terms of the Treaty of Lahore were being carried out in the spirit which the ward of the British Government was warranted to expect.

How easily might the Government at this period have finally settled matters with the Maharajah in a manner satisfactory to him and creditable to themselves!

Between 1862 and 1882 many transactions took place between the Maharajah and Government, relative to the purchase of estates and advances of money for various purposes, a detailed statement of which is given further on, in quotations from the book published by the Maharajah in 1884.

No public attention was drawn to the conditions of affairs until August, 1882, when Duleep Singh, no doubt observing the action of the Government in South Africa with regard to Cetewayo, commenced the following correspondence in the *Times:*—

THE CLAIMS OF AN INDIAN PRINCE

To The Editor Of *The Times*

Aug. 31st, 1882

SIR,

As the era of doing justice and restoration appears to have dawned, judging from the recent truly liberal and noble act of the present Liberal Government, headed now by the great Gladstone the Just, I am encouraged to lay before the British nation, through the medium of *The Times,* the injustice which I have suffered, in the hope that, although generosity may not be lavished upon me to the

55

same extent as has been bestowed upon King Cetewayo, yet that some magnanimity might be shown towards me by this great Christian Empire.

When I succeeded to the throne of the Punjab I was only an infant, and the Khalsa soldiery, becoming more and more mutinous and overbearing during both my uncle's and my mother's Regencies, at last, unprovoked, crossed the Sutlej and attacked the friendly British Power, and was completely defeated and entirely routed by the English army.

Had, at that time, my dominions been annexed to the British territories, I would have now not a word to say; for I was, at that time, an independent chief at the head of an independent people, and any penalty which might have been then inflicted would have been perfectly just; but that kind, true English gentleman, the late Lord Hardinge, in consideration of the friendship which had existed between the British Empire and the "Lion of the Punjab", replaced me on my throne, and the diamond Koh-i-noor on my arm, at one of the Durbars. The Council of Regency, which was then created to govern the country during my minority, finding that it was not in their power to rule the Punjab unaided, applied for assistance to the representative of the British Government, who, after stipulating for absolute power to control every Government department, entered into the Bhyrowal Treaty with me, by which it was guaranteed that I should be protected on my throne until I attained the age of sixteen years, the British also furnishing troops both for the above object and preservation of peace in the country, in consideration of a certain sum to be paid to them annually by my Durbar for the maintenance of that force.

Thus the British nation, with open eyes, assumed my guardianship, the nature of which is clearly defined in a proclamation subsequently issued by Lord Hardinge's orders, on the 20th August, 1847, which declares that the tender age of the Maharajah Duleep Singh causes him to feel the interest of a father in the education and guardianship of the young Prince.—(*Vide* *"Punjab Papers"* at the British Museum).

Two English officers, carrying letters bearing my signature, were despatched by the British Resident, in conjunction with my Durbar, to take possession of the fortress of Mooltan and the surrounding district in my name; but my servant Moolraj, refusing to acknowledge my authority, caused them to be put to death; whereupon, both the late Sir F.Currie and the brave Sir Herbert Edwardes most urgently requested the Commander-in-Chief of the British forces at Simla, as there were not sufficient English soldiers at Lahore at the time, to send some European troops without delay, in order to crush this rebellion in the bud, as they affirmed that the consequences could not be calculated which might follow, if it were allowed to spread; but the late Lord Gough, with the concurrence of the late Marquis of Dalhousie, refused to comply with their wishes, alleging the unhealthiness of the season as his reason for doing so.

My case at that time was exactly similar to what the Khedive's is at this moment; Arabi being, in his present position to his master, what Moolraj was to me—viz., a rebel.

At last, very tardily, the British Government sent troops (as has been done in Egypt) to quell the rebellion, which had by that time vastly increased in the Punjab, and who entered my territories, headed by a proclamation, issued by Lord Dalhousie's orders, to the following effect:-

Inclosure 8 in No. 42—To the subjects, servants, and dependants of the Lahore State, and residents of all classes and castes, whither Sikhs, Mussalmans, or others, within the territories of Maharajah Duleep Singh......Whereas certain evil-disposed persons and traitors have excited rebellion and insurrection, and have seduced portions of the population of the Punjab from their allegiance, and have raised an armed opposition to the British authority; and whereas the condign punishment of the insurgents is necessary.... therefore the British army, under the command of the Right Hon. the Commander-in-Chief, has entered the Punjab districts. The army will not return to its cantonments until full punishment of all insurgents has been effected, all opposition to the constituted authority put down, and obedience and order have been re-established.

Thus it is clear from the above that the British Commander-in-Chief did not enter my dominions as a conqueror, nor the army to stay there, and, therefore, it is not correct to assert, as some do, that the Punjab was a military conquest.

And whereas it is not the desire of the British Government

that those who are innocent of the above offences, who have taken no part, secretly or openly, in the disturbances, and who have remained faithful in their obedience to the Government of Maharajah Duleep Singh.... should suffer with the guilty.

But after order was restored, and finding only a helpless child to deal with, the temptation being too strong, Lord Dalhousie annexed the Punjab, and instead of carrying out the solemn compact entered into by the British Government at Bhyrowal, sold almost all my personal as well as all my private property, consisting of jewels, gold and silver plate, even some of my wearing apparel and household furniture, and distributed the proceeds, amounting (I was told) to £250,000, as prize money among those very troops who had come to put down rebellion against my authority.

Thus I, the innocent, who never lifted up even my little finger against the British Government, was made to suffer in the same manner with my own subjects who would not acknowledge my authority, in spite of the declaration of the above-quoted proclamation, that it is not the desire of the British Government that the innocent should suffer with the guilty.

Lord Dalhousie, in writing to the Secret Committee of the late Court of Directors, in order to justify his unjust act, among other arguments employs the following. He says:—

It has been objected that the present dynasty in the Punjab cannot with justice be subverted, since the Maharajah Duleep Singh, being yet a minor, can hardly be held responsible for the acts of the nation. With deference to those by whom these views have been entertained, I must dissent entirely from the soundness of this doctrine. It is, I venture to think, altogether untenable as a principle; it has been disregarded heretofore in practice, and disregarded in the case of the Maharajah Duleep Singh. When in 1845 the Khalsa army invaded our territories, the Maharajah was not held to be free from responsibility, nor was he exempted from the consequences of the acts of the people. On the contrary, the Government of India confiscated to itself the richest provinces of the Maharajah's kingdom, and was applauded for the moderation which had exacted no more. If the Maharajah was not exempted from responsibility on the plea of his tender years at the age of eight, he cannot on that plea be entitled to exemption from a like responsibility now that he is three years older.

But in thus arguing, his Lordship became blind to the fact that in 1845, when the Khalsa army invaded the British territories, I was an independent chief, but after the ratification of the Bhyrowal Treaty I was made the ward of the British nation; and how could I, under these circumstances, be held responsible for the neglect of my guardians in not crushing Moolraj's rebellion at once, the necessity of doing which was clearly and repeatedly pointed out by the British Resident at Lahore?

Again, his Lordship says, "The British Government has rigidly observed the obligations which the Treaty imposed on them, and fully acted up to the spirit and letter of its contract." No doubt all this was or may have been true, except so far that neither peace was preserved in the country nor I protected on my throne till I attained the age of sixteen years—two very important stipulations of that Treaty.

He further alleges, "In return for the aid of the British troops they (my Durbar) bound themselves to pay to us a subsidy of twenty-two lakhs (£220,000) per annum........from the day when that Treaty was signed to the present hour, not one rupee has ever been paid."

Now, the above statement is not correct, because of the following despatch which exists:-"Enclosure No. 5, in No. 23", the Acting Resident at Lahore affirms, "The Durbar has paid into this treasury gold to the value of Rs. 13,56,637 0.6." (£135,837 14s. 1d., taking the value of a rupee at 2s.).

Likewise Lord Dalhousie alludes to Sirdar Chutter Singh's conduct. Enclosure 19 in No. 36 will show those who care to look for it, the reprimand which Captain Abbott then received from the Resident for his treatment of that chief, who, after that, with his sons, without doubt believed that the Bhyrowal Treaty was not going to be carried out; and, judging from the events which followed, were they right in their views, or were they not ?

(1) Thus I have been most unjustly deprived of my kingdom, yielding, as shown by Lord Dalhousie's own computation in (I think) 1850, a surplus revenue of some £500,000, and no doubt now vastly exceeds that sum.

(2) I have also been prevented, unjustly, from receiving the rentals of my private estates (*vide* Prinsep's *"History of the Sikhs,"*

compiled for the Government of India) in the Punjab, amounting to some £130,000 per annum, since 1849, although my private property is not confiscated by the terms of the annexation which I was compelled to sign by my guardians when I was a minor, and therefore, I presume, it is an illegal document, and I am still the lawful Sovereign of the Punjab; but this is of no moment, for I am quite content to be the subject of my most gracious Sovereign, no matter how it was brought about, for her graciousness towards me has been boundless.

(3) All my personal property has also been taken from me, excepting £20,000 worth, which I was informed by the late Sir John Login was permitted to be taken with me to Futtehghur when I was exiled; and the rest, amounting to some £250,000, disposed of as stated before. What is still more unjust in my case is, that most of my servants who remained faithful to me, were permitted to retain all their landed estates (or *jagheers*), given to them by me and my predecessors, whereas I, their master, who did not even lift up my little finger against the British nation, was not considered worthy to be treated on the same footing of equality with them, because, I suppose, my sin being that I happened to be the ward of a Christian Power.

The enormous British liberality permits a life stipend of £25,000 per annum, which is reduced by certain charges (known to the proper authorities) to some £13,000, to be paid to me from the revenues of India.

Lately, an Act of Parliament has been passed, by which, some months hence, the munificent sum of £2,000 will be added to my above stated available income, but on the absolute condition that my estates must be sold at my death, thus causing my dearly-loved English home to be broken up, and compelling my descendants to seek some other asylum.

A very meagre provision, considering of what, and how, I have been deprived, has also been made for my successors.

If one righteous man was found in the two most wicked cities of the world, I pray God that at least one honourable, just, and noble Englishman may be forthcoming out of this Christian land of liberty and justice to advocate my cause in Parliament; otherwise, what chance have I of obtaining justice, considering that my despoiler, guardian, judge, advocate, and jury, is the British nation itself?

Generous and Christian Englishmen, accord me a just and liberal treatment, for the sake of the fair name of your nation, of which I have now the honour to be a naturalized member, for it is more blessed to give than to take.

I have the honour to remain, Sir,

Your most obliged servant,

DULEEP SINGH

Eleveden Hall, Thetfort, Suffolk,

Aug. 28th, 1882.

It will be acknowledged that there is nothing in the tone or spirit of the above letter to justify the contemptuous reply which it received, contained in the following leading article printed in *The Times* of August 31st, 1882, and which bears conclusive evidence of official inspiration. Considering the rank then held by the Maharajah in England, the consideration due to him on account of the position from which we had deposed him, and his own known loyalty and attachment to the person of the Sovereign, surely a more dignified and less irritating response might have been afforded him! To try and turn a man into ridicule is no answer to a specific charge, and the real point at issue is, in this article, merely fenced with.

THE "TIMES" — *Aug. 31st,* 1882

Encouraged, as it would seem, by the restoration of Cetewayo, Maharajah Duleep Singh puts forward an impassioned plea for the consideration of his own claims. On a first glance, his letter reads as if he demanded nothing less than to be replaced on the throne of the Punjab. He professes to establish his right to that position and then to waive it, magnanimously avowing that he is quite content to be the subject of his most gracious Sovereign, whose graciousness towards him had been boundless. His real object, however, is far less ambitious. It is to prefer a claim for a more generous treatment of his private affairs at the hands of the Indian Government. In lieu of the sovereignty of the Punjab, with its unbounded power and unlimited resources, "the enormous British liberality," he complains, permits him only a life stipend of £25,000 per annum, which is reduced by certain charges to some £13,000. All that he has hitherto succeeded in obtaining from the Indian Government is an arrangement, lately sanctioned by Act of Parliament, whereby he will receive an addition of £2,000 to his annual income on condition that his estates are sold at his death in order to liquidate his liabilities, and provide for his widow and children. It is really against this arrangement that the Maharajah appeals. His argument concerning his *de jure* sovereignty of the Punjab is manifestly only intended to support his pecuniary claims. If these were settled to his satisfaction, he would doubtless be content, and more than content, to die, as he has lived, an English country gentleman, with estates swarming with game, and with an income sufficient for his needs. This is a sort of appeal to its justice and generosity with which the English public is not unfamiliar. Duleep Singh is not the first dispossessed Eastern Prince who has felt himself aggrieved by the dispositions of the Indian Government, nor is this the first occasion on which his own claim have been heard of. For a long time he preferred a claim for the Koh-i-noor, of which he alleged that he had been wrongfully despoiled . Now it is his private estates in India which he declares have been confiscated without adequate compensation. No one, of course, would wish that a prince in the Maharajah's position should be ungenerously treated . He is, as it were, a ward of the English nation, and even his extravagances might be leniently regarded. But as the claim, now publicly preferred by the Maharajah, has been disallowed after full consideration by successive Governments both in India and this country it may not be amiss to show that his case is by no means so strong as he still affects to consider it .

The events of two Sikh wars, and their sequal, have probably faded out of the memory of most of our readers. They are, however, accurately stated, so far as the main facts are concerned in the Maharajah's letter. It is not so much with those facts

62

themselves that we are now concerned as with the Maharajah's inferences from them, and with certain other facts which he has not found it convenient to state. It is perfectly true that after the overthrow of the "Khalsa" power in the sanguinary battle of Sobraon, Lord Hardinge declined to annex the Punjab and replaced the Maharajah on the throne under the Regency of his mother, the Ranee, assisted by a Council of Sirdars. This settlement, however, proved a failure, and was replaced by the arrangement made under the Bhyrowal Treaty, whereby the entire control and guidance of affairs was vested in the British Resident, and the presence of British troops was guaranteed until the Maharajah should attain his majority.

The second Sikh war, which began with the revolt of Moolraj in 1848, soon proved the futility of this arrangement also, and after the surrender of Mooltan and the battle of Gujrat, which finally broke the reviving power of the Khalsa, Lord Dalhousie, who had succeeded Lord Hardinge as Governor-General, decided that the time had come for the incorporation of the Punjab with the British Dominions in India. Duleep Singh was at this time only eleven years of age; but he had been recognized for more than three years as the Sovereign of the Punjab, and by the advice of his Durbar at Lahore he signed the terms of settlement proposed by the British Commissioner, whereby he renounced "for himself, his heirs, and his successors, all right, title, and claim to the sovereignty of the Punjab, or to any sovereign power whatever." By subsequent clauses of the same instrument "all the property of the State, of whatever description and wheresoever found, was confiscated to the East India Company; the Koh-i-noor was surrendered to the Queen of England; a pension of not less than four, and not exceeding five lakhs of rupees was secured to the Maharajah, "for the support of himself, his relatives, and the servants of the State," and the Company undertook to treat the Maharajah with respect and honour, and to allow him to retain the title of "Maharajah Duleep Singh, Bahadoor." Of this instrument, the Maharajah now says that he was compelled to sign it by his guardians when he was a minor, and he argues that the political necessity which dictated it was due to the laches of the Indian Government, which had failed to fulfil the pledges of the Bhyrowal Treaty, and had allowed the revolt of Moolraj to develop into a Sikh rebellion. In answer to these allegations, it is sufficent to quote the report of the British Commissioner, who presented the terms for signature. "The paper," he says, "was then handed to the Maharajah, who immediately affixed his signature. The alacrity with which he took the papers when offered, was a matter of remark to all, and suggested the idea that possibly he had been instructed by his advisers that any show of hesitation might lead to the substitution of terms less favourable than those which he had been offered." Moreover, the plea that the Maharajah was a minor, and therefore not a free agent, is fatal to his own case; he was two years younger when the Bhyrowal Treaty was signed, and younger still when the settlement of Lord Hardinge replaced him on the throne, and restored to him the sovereignty, which he even now acknowledges might at that time have been rightly forfeited. We need not dwell on this point, however. The Maharajah himself would hardly press it. His claim of sovereignty is merely intended to cover his claim for money. He never was much more than nominal Sovereign of the Punjab, and he probably desires nothing so little at this moment as the restitution of his sovereign rights. The political question has long been closed; it only remains to consider whether the personal and financial question still remains open. The Maharajah complains that he was deprived of his personal and private property—with insignificant exceptions—and of the rentals of his landed estates. There is, however, no mention of private property in the terms of settlement accepted by the Maharajah; and a minute of Lord Dalhousie, recorded in 1855, states explicitly that at the time the Punjab was annexed, the youth had no territories, no lands, no property, to which he could succeed. The pension accorded by the East India Company was plainly intended to support the Maharajah in becoming state, and to provide for his personal dependants; and the British Government expressly reserved to itself the right of allotting only such portion as it thought fit of the "Four Lakh Fund," as the pension was called, to the Maharajah's personal use. So long ago as 1853, Lord Dalhousie wrote a despatch, intended to remove from the Maharajah's mind all idea that the Four Lakh

Fund would ultimately revert to himself, and characterizing such an idea as "entirely erroneous."

The Indian Government, however, has certainly not dealt ungenerously with the Maharajah. It is true that it has not recognized his claim to certain private estates no record of which exists, still less has it listened to any of his attempts to assail the validity of the instrument whereby his sovereignty was extinguished. For some years after the annexation, his personal allowance out of the Four Lakh Fund was fixed at £12,500 a year— a sum which was considered entirely satisfactory by the leading Ministers of the Durbar, which assented and advised the Maharajah to assent to the terms of 1849. But in 1859 this allowance was doubled, and the Maharajah himself more than once acknowledged in subsequent years the liberality of the arrangements made. The allowance of £25,000 a year has been reduced to the £13,000 mentioned by the the Maharajah in his letter, not by any act of the Indian Government, but by what, if he were only an English Country Gentleman, we should be compelled to call extravagance, though, as he is an Eastern Prince, it is more generous, perhaps, to describe it as magnificence. He first bought a property in Gloucestershire, but this was sold some years ago, and his present estate at Elveden, in Suffolk, was purchased for £138,000, the money being advanced by the Government, and interest for the loan to the amount of £5,664 per annum being paid by the Maharajah. Some two or three years ago the Home Government of India proposed to release the Maharajah from payment of this annual sum provided that he would consent to the sale of the estate, either at once or at his death, for the repayment of the principal of the loans advanced. This proposal, however, was rejected by the Indian Government, which maintained, in very strong and plain language, that the Maharajah had already been treated with exceptional liberality, and that if he wanted more money he should sell his estate. The Indian Government remained inexorable, but the liberality, of the Home Government was not yet exhausted . The Maharajah had built a house at Elveden, at a cost of £60,000, and had borrowed £40,000 from a London banking firm for the purpose. For this loan £2,000 interest had to be paid, and the India

Office has lately sanctioned the repayment of the capital sum without making any further charge on the Maharajah. It is to this arrangement, and to the Act of Parliament which sanctions it, that the Maharajah refers with some bitterness at the close of his letter. In order to settle his affairs, and to provide for his wife and family, the Act of Parliament requires that his estate at Elveden should be sold after his death. An argument which starts from the sovereign claims of the son of the "Lion of the Punjab," ends, somewhat ridiculously, though not without a touch of pathos, with the sorrows of the Squire of Elveden. Duleep Singh began life as a Maharajah of the Punjab, with absolute power and boundless wealth if he had only been old enough to enjoy them, and if the Khalsa would only have allowed him to do so. He is not even allowed to end it as an English country gentleman leaving an encumbered estate and an embarrassed heir. There is really a certain tragedy about the whole matter. Fate and the British Power have deprived the Maharajah of the sovereignty to which he was born. He has done his best to become an English squire; and if he has lived beyond his income, he may plead abundance of examples in the class to which he has attached himself; yet he is forced to bear the consequences himself, and not to inflict them on his children and descendants, as an English squire would be able to do. The whole case is one which it is very difficult to judge upon any abstract principles. It is, no doubt, the duty of every man to live within his income, and yet if the Maharajah has failed to acquire a virtue rare indeed among Eastern princes and not too common in the class to which he belongs by adoption, there is no Englishman but would feel ashamed if he or his descendants were thereby to come to want. At the same time it is impossible for the Indian Government, which has claims on his slender resources far more urgent than those of the magnificient squire of Elveden, to guarantee him indefinitely against the consequences of his own improvidence. At any rate, it is safe to warn him against encumbering his personal claims by political pleas which are wholly inadmissible. He is very little likely to excite sympathy for his pecuniary troubles by his bold, but scarcely successful, attempt to show that if he could only come by his own, he is still the lawful Sovereign of the Punjab.

66

THE CLAIMS OF THE MAHARAJAH DULEEP SINGH

To the Editor of *"The Times"*

SIR,

As your leading article of Thursday, the 31st ult., commenting on my letter of the 28th, which you were so good as to publish, contains many inaccuracies as to matters of fact, which no one, perhaps, can correct so precisely as myself, I trust you will allow me to do so, and to make a few observations.

(1) You say: "All that he has hitherto succeeded in obtaining from the Indian Government, is an arrangement, lately sanctioned by Act of Parliament, whereby he will receive an addition of £2,000 to his annual income, on condition that his estates are sold at his death, in order to liquidate his liabilities, and provide for his widow and children. It is really against this arrangement that the Maharajah appeals."

I do *not* "really appeal" against the above arrangement, but what I do certainly think unjust in it is, that I am not permitted to repay, during my life, the loan which is to be made under it—£16,000 having already been advanced to me—and that I am thus forbidden to preserve, by a personal sacrifice, their English home to my descendants. In April last I sent a cheque for £3,542 14s., representing capital and compound interest at the rate of five per cent to the India Office, but it was returned to me.

My widow and children, should I leave any, were already provided for, under arrangements which existed before this Act was passed.

(2) With reference to your quotation from the British Commissioner, as to my "alacrity" in signing the terms, I have simply to say that, being then a child, I did not understand what I was signing.

(3) "Moreover" you say, "the plea that the Maharajah was a minor, and, therefore, not a free agent, is fatal to his own case; he was two years younger when the Bhyrowal Treaty was signed, and younger still when the settlement of Lord Hardinge replaced him on the throne, and restored to him the sovereignty which he even now acknowledges, might at that time have been rightly forfeited. We do not dwell on this point, however. The Maharajah himself would hardly press it."

But, whether it is fatal to my case or not, I *do* press it, and maintain that after the ratification of the Bhyrowal Treaty, I was a *ward of the British nation,* and that it was unjust on the part of the guardian to deprive me of my kingdom, in consequence of a failure in the guardianship.

Here are Lord Hardinge's own words: "But, in addition to these considerations of a political nature, the Governor-General is bound to be guided by the obligations which the British Government has contracted when it consented to be the guardian of the young Prince during his minority" (*vide* p. 49, *"Punjab Papers,"* 1847-49).

(4) "The Maharajah complains," you would say, "that he was deprived of his personal

and private property—with insignificant exceptions—and of the rentals of his landed estates. There is, however, no mention of private property in the terms of the settlement accepted by the Maharajah; and a minute of Lord Dalhousie, recorded in 1855, explicitly states that at the time the Punjab was annexed, the youth had no territories, no lands, no property to which he could succeed." My reply is, that at the time of the annexation I had succeeded to territories, lands, and personal property, and was in possession, and these possessions were held in trust, and managed for me, under treaty, by the British Government.

That I had succeeded and was possessed of private estates in land, is an historical fact, and a matter of public records. Moreover, these estates had belonged to my family, one of them having being acquired by marriage, before my father attained to sovereignty. The statement in Lord Dalhousie's minute only amounts to denial of the existence of the sun by a blind man; and there are none so blind as those who will not see.

And now with regard to my alleged extravagance, these are the facts. The life stipend of £25,000 allotted to me, has to bear the following deductions:— (1) £5,664 interest, payable to the Government of India; (2) about £3,000 as premium on policies of insurance of my life, executed in order to add to the meagre provision made for my descendants by the British Government, and as security for the loan from my bankers; (3) £1,000 per annum for two pensions of £500 per annum each to the widows of the superintendent appointed by Lord Dalhousie to take charge of me after the annexation, and of my kind friend, the late controller of my establishment; besides which there is some £300 per annum payable in pensions to old servants in India.

In order to be able to receive His Royal Highness the Prince of Wales, and to return the hospitality of men in my own position of life, and because I was advised and considered—not I think, unreasonably—that the rank granted to me by Her Majesty required it to be done, I expended some £22,000 (not £60,000, as you were informed) in alterations and repairs to the old house on this estate; suitable furniture cost £8,000 more.

At a cost of some £3,000, I have purchased life annuities, to be paid to the before-mentioned widow ladies, in case they should survive me.

About £8,000 more had to be borrowed from my bankers on mortgage, to complete the purchase of this estate, as the money lent me by the Government of India was insufficient by that amount. Thus, my debts amount to something like £44,000, of which £30,000 is covered by policies of insurance, £8,000 by mortgage, and the remainder amply secured by personal assets. Therefore, instead of my estates being heavily encumbered, my heirs, were I to die at this moment, would succeed to a house and furniture which are worth much more than £30,000, without any liability, besides some £70,000, secured by insurance on my life.

I think you are bound to acquit the Squire of Elveden of extravagance.

When the agricultural depression set in, I requested the Home Government to make an allowance that would enable me to maintain my position, and they kindly, after causing all the accounts to be examined, helped me with £10,000, but did not accuse me of extravagance. Subsequently, pending the consideration of my affairs, some £6,000 or £7,000 more was advanced to pay off pressing bills, as during that time I had not completed the arrangements for reducing my establishment. Out of the above loan about £10,000 was invested in live and dead stock on farms in hand, and would be forthcoming, if demanded, at a very short notice.

Thus the extravagance during my residence at Elveden is reduced to the fabulous sum of some £12,000, and I possess enough personally, beyond any question, to discharge debts to that amount, and some £6,000 more, should they exist at my death.

In common justice, therefore, Mr. Editor, I ask you to enable me to contradict, in as prominent a manner as they were brought forward in your most influential journal, the rumours as to my extravagance.

In the first paragraph of your leading article of Thursday, the 31st ult., you say, "that the claim now publicly preferred by the Maharajah has been disallowed after full consideration by successive Governments, both in India and this country." Yes, it is very easy to disallow a claim without hearing the real claimant.

The English law grants the accused the chance of proving himself not guilty; but I am condemned unheard: is this just?

I remain, Sir, your most obliged,

DULEEP SINGH

Elveden Hall, Thetford, Suffolk,

Sept. 6th, 1882.

The Maharajah then, finding no notice taken of his appeal, devoted himself to compiling, with the assistance of his solicitor, a book which was published in June, 1884, "for the information of his friends, and to disabuse their minds of any prejudice which may have arisen from what appeared in print about a year ago."

The following extracts from the above-mentioned book will give the situation from the Maharajah's point of view:—

By the Treaty of Bhyrowal, in December, 1846, the British Government became the guardian of the infant Prince, and caused his mother to be removed from his vicinity, on account of the influence she was likely to exert over him, and her well-known character for intrigue.

In 1849 the Treaty of Lahore put an end to the Protectorate, but by it the British Government entered into an engagement with the Maharajah to pay him a pension, and took entire charge of his person, exercising a full control over his movements, expenditure, education, and associates, appointing Dr. Login as superintendent under the direction of the Governor-General.

They also undertook the administration of his pension, fixing the amount to be paid to him, to his relatives and dependants, as it was certainly necessary for some one to act for him in this matter until he came of age.

There was a further complication in the matter.

The Government, as is known, in 1849, took possession of all the property of the Maharajah, both in lands and money. The Treaty gave them all the *State property*, therefore, they became trustees for the Maharajah as to his private property. Disputes have since arisen how much, and which portions of the property are of one kind, and how much, and which portions are of the other kind—and there is also a difference of opinion about the *duration* of the entire pension under the words of the Treaty—so that there are several points of conflict between the Government and its ward.

The Government claims to be the sole arbiter on these conflicting questions, and hitherto has uniformly decided them in its own favour, never rendering any account of its stewardship. Between private individuals, a Chancery judge would interfere, and would appoint trustees, &c., and investigate the case before deciding it; in the meantime, the funds would be secured, and set aside at interest, for the benefit of the successful party in the litigation.

In this case, however, the Government has remained master of the situation. The Maharajah has been advised that the courts of law are, in all probability, powerless to decide between him and the Government, and the latter keeps possession.

It will be interesting here to insert the views of the Government, as embodied in minutes by Lord Dalhousie in 1856, and by Sir Charles Wood in 1860.

Lord Dalhousie's *Minute.*

When the Maharajah quitted India, the object which the Superintendent had in view, was to obtain for His Highness a grant of land in the Eastern Dhoon, near Derayli, with the expectation, I presume, that the Maharajah would live at Mussoorie during the hot season, as he had been in the habit of doing; and would occupy himself, and interest himself, in the cultivation and improvement of the estate which was to be granted to him.

The Superintendent appeared to be under the impression that the Maharajah himself very strongly desired the settlement of his future position. It seemed to me very unlikely that a boy of his years would have a strong feeling of any kind on such a subject, and quite certain that he could not as yet know his own mind.

In correspondence with Dr. Login since the Maharajah has resided in England, I have learnt that upon being further questioned upon the subject, His Highness did not seem to desire an estate at all, but preferred a money stipend, and spoke as if he were under the impression that the four lakhs which were mentioned in the paper of terms, and which were granted on the annexation of the Punjab, would all ultimately lapse to him. The view which was taken by His Highness of this subject was entirely erroneous.

The terms granted did not secure to the Maharajah four lakhs, out of which His Highness was to grant pensions to relatives and followers, which, on the death of the recipients, were to revert to the Maharajah. The terms simply set apart four lakhs of rupees at the time of annexation, as provision for the Maharajah, for the members of his family, and servants of the State.

Minute of the Council of India

By Sir Charles Wood, K.C.B. *March 21st,* 1860.

At the close of the second Sikh war, it was determined to annex the Punjab to British territory, and to put an end to the separate Khalsa Government of the Sikhs. The form in which the arrangement for this purpose was recorded, was a paper of terms granted and accepted at Lahore in 1849, and notified by the Governor-General.

The provisions in favour of the Maharajah are contained in the 4th and 5th Articles of those terms (the first three all being declaratory of the surrender) as follows:—

"4th. His Highness Duleep Singh shall receive from the Honourable East India Company, for the support of himself, his relatives, and the servants of the state, a pension not less than four, and not exceeding five, lakhs of Company's rupees per annum.

"5th. His Highness shall be treated with respect and honour. He shall retain the title of Maharajah Duleep Singh Bahadoor; and he shall continue to receive, during his life, such portion of the above-named pension as may be allowed to himself personally, provided he shall remain obedient to the British Government, and reside at such place as the Governor-General of India may select."

The terms were signed by the young Maharajah, and by six of the principal Sirdars and people of his court.

The first question is, what are the Maharajah's rights under the two articles, and what are the obligations which the Government of India came under towards him personally?

It is clear that, being a minor, required to live where the Governor-General might determine, he was not intended to be the recipient of the "pension not less than four, and not exceeding five, lakhs of Company's rupees per annum," which was to form the provision for "himself, his relatives," and "the servants of the State."

This Article, though using his name as the head of the State at the time the announcement was made, must be construed with the following Article, which provides that "he shall continue to receive, during his life, such portion of the above-named *pension* as may be allotted to himself personally," under the condition of good behaviour.

The personal claim of the Maharajah is here limited to the receipt, for his life, of his *personal* stipend; and the amount to be allotted to him was left entirely to the Government of India.

During the first years of the Maharajah's minority the annual sum allotted for his personal allowance was 120,000 rupees per annum. It was afterwards increased to 150,000 per annum; the increase taking effect from the date of his attaining the age of eighteen.

The Indian Government recommended that, on his attaining the age of twenty-one, £25,000 should be allotted as his personal allowance. This sum, together with the present sums allotted to the other recipients of allowances, under the 4th Article, will exceed the amount of four lakhs.

Some of these allowances will necessarily fall in sooner or later; and the amount of allowances will again be reduced below four lakhs.

A question may arise as to the obligations under the terms of 1849, as to the disposal of any such annual sums falling in.

The Maharajah seems to expect that he may be considered entitled to benefit from such lapses. But this claim has been distinctly negatived by Lord Dalhousie, who cannot be mistaken as to the meaning of the terms which he granted; and the provision that the Maharajah shall only receive what may be specially allotted to him, is so clear in the 5th Article, that he can evidently have no rights to any increase of his stipend consequently.

It is evident that the portion of the pension allotted to others

72

can only be for their respective lives.

The provision in the Maharajah's favour is only for life. This is expressly provided for.

It cannot be supposed that the allowances to be assigned to the other persons were for any other term than that assigned for the Maharajah's, namely, for their respective lives. The only other possible construction of the terms would be, that the allowances of the other parties were to be for the period of the Maharajah's life.

But it would be an absurdity to suppose because the 4th Article uses the Maharajah's name as the recipient of the entire provision, that the pensions assigned to other members of the family and State servants would at once have ceased if the Maharajah had happened to die during his minority. All of them, like the personal stipend of the Maharajah, must be regarded as assured life stipends, but not extending beyond life.

The amount, therefore, of any stipends so falling in hereafter, must, according to the terms of 1849, fall into the British Government.

There is no doubt, however, but that, upto the present time, the difference between the sums allotted to the Maharajah, his relatives, and the servants of the State, and the amount of four lakhs, which was the smallest sum which it was provided that the British Government should apply to the purposes mentioned, has not been so expended. What the amount of such accumulation is we have no means of ascertaining in England; but it is understood that there may be a balnace of between £150,000 and £200,000.

Tha Maharajah supposes he is entitled to claim this as payable to himself personally; first, because the 4th Article of the terms of 1849, uses his name as recipient of the whole four lakhs; and secondly, because he alleges that the balance is composed mainly, if not entirely, of short payment to himself, of what he considers to have been due to him during his minority.

The simple answer to this claim is afforded by the 5th Article, which specifically provides that he is only to receive the "portion of the above-named pension" that might be allotted to "himself personally," and the Government of India might allot to him whatever sum it thought proper, as it might in a like manner to the other persons referred to in the 4th Article. Any part of the £40,000 per annum which has not been allotted, and has accumulated in the Treasury of the British Government, is at their disposal; but they are bound to apply it for the purposes stated in the terms of 1849.

It is a fair question, however, what is the best method of disposing of any balance that the British Government has now in its hands, and which it is under obligation to spend for the benefit of these parties; and it would certainly seem that the most appropriate disposition will be to make a provision for the families of the life stipendiaries.

It is to be observed that it is the practice in India, in dealing with political stipendiaries, to leave the provision for the family to be settled after the stipendiary's decease, and not to place in the hands of the annuitant.

The Maharajah has felt the precarious position in which any family which he might leave would be placed in this respect, and has asked us to give him security on this point.

The Committee of the Council proposed a scheme on this especial point, namely, that a sum should be capitalized, sufficient to produce an annual sum of £10,000 per annum, as a permanent income after his death for his widow and any children he might leave.

The Maharajah has asked for permission to bequeath this amount for some public purposes for the Punjab, in case he should die childless; but to this the Committee have refused to accede.

By the terms of 1849, as already shown, the Maharajah is only entitled to receive for life such sum as may be allotted to him. The Committee, however, were most willing to remove his natural anxiety, by enabling him to make a liberal provision for his wife and children after his death.

But they could not consistently with their sense of duty place at his disposal, by will, any funds for any other purpose. If funds should be available for public purposes, their application must rest with the Government.

The Committee further said that, if the Maharajah should prefer to receive at once such a proportion of the present accumulation as the Government of India may consider it proper to grant to him, with

74

reference to the claims of all others interested, there can be no objection to that amount being paid to him down, leaving him to make his own arrangements for his family, which, in that case, would have no claim to look to the Government for any further provision after his decease. If the Maharajah prefers this to the offer of capitalizing a sum producing £10,000 per annum as a trust-fund, for the benefit of his family, the case will be referred to the Governor-General of India, desiring him to ascertain what the real balance of unappropriated "pension" payable under the 4th Article of the Terms of 1849 now is—and also to determine the proportion of that balance which may fairly be assigned to the Maharajah. This is strictly conformable with those terms.

The Council of India are of opinion that the proposal to capitalize the proportion of the stipend of £25,000 per annum, *i.e.,* £10,000 per annum, as a trust provision for his family, is the most beneficial arrangement for the Maharajah. They will, however, willingly accede to whichever of these arrangements he may prefer.

On the foregoing the Maharajah's remarks:—

The reader will see that the Government is of opinion that it is under no obligation to give, during the Maharajah's life, any larger pension than it may choose to allow, nor to give any pension to his family after his death.

The Maharajah does not agree to this as a true interpretation of the Treaty, nor, we think, would ordinary minds come to that conclusion.

It is admitted that the pension is not entirely to cease with the life of the Maharajah, but as to certain portions, it is to be continued after his death for certain purposes. It is also stated that the name of the Maharajah is used in the 4th Article of the Treaty, not in the individual capacity, but as "head of the State."

This reading favours the construction for which the Maharajah contends, viz., that the pension was to be hereditary, and that any forfeiture that he might incur would not prejudice the rights of his children.

The Maharajah does not believe that it could have been intended

75

to confine his compensation to a mere life pension in exchange for an hereditary estate of not less than two millions sterling per annum, which increases constantly with the prosperity of the country.

At all events, the interpretation put upon the Treaty by the Government is so unfavourable to the Maharajah, and to his posterity, and so different from what, we venture to say, an ordinary reader would gather from its perusal—so different from what must have been understood by the assembled chiefs in 1849, when they heard it read by Sir Henry Elliot—that, if correct, it requires some more impartial sanction and confirmation than that of a Government department to render it acceptable or satisfactory to the Maharajah.

If it were really intended after the Treaty to leave the Maharajah and his descendants entirely at the mercy of the British Government; if the Government also intended to absorb all his personal and private property, as well as to deprive him of his personal freedom, why ask him to sign any treaty at all? He was fully in the power of the British Government and army, who might have disposed of him at pleasure.

We cannot think that the India Office have rightly interpreted either the language or the spirit of the Treaty; but we unhesitatingly say that, if the Treaty does mean what Sir Charles Wood stated in his memorandum, it is a document which must excite feelings of just indignation in every honest mind.

As a consequence of its interpretations, as explained above, the Maharajah has never had what he considers to be the full benefit of the Treaty of 1849; and, moreover, he has, under cover of the Treaty, been deprived of private property and lands which it did not profess to confiscate.

Taking a lakh of rupees to be equal to £10,000, the pension would be between £40,000 and £50,000 (say £45,000).

The payments actually made to the Maharajah are as follows:—

From 1849 to 1856	...	...	£12,000 per annum
" 1856 to 1858	...	...	£15,000 "
" 1858 onwards	...	....	£25,000 "

Besides these payments, allowances to relatives and dependants to the extent of £18,000 per annum at the commencement (1849) which were reduced to £15,000 in 1859 have been made. These allowances have rapidly dwindled into a very small sum, if indeed

76

they have not vanished altogether.

In 1859 about £100,000 was the aggregate saving of the Government on the four lakhs.

In 1862 the Government provided a sum of £105,000 (which probably was the exact amount saved, but they endeavoured to make it appear as a voluntary provision made by them), for the purchase of an estate, to be settled on the Maharajah and his issue, also empowering him to bequeath to his legitimate offspring a sum of four per cent. India Capital Stock, to be provided by Government, this amount to be sufficient to yield an income of £7,000 per annum, subsequently increased to £10,800 per annum.

Between 1862 and 1882 the Government advanced the sum of £198,000, charged on the India Capital Stock, and (in the event of his leaving no issue) on the Suffolk estates.

Of this, £60,000 was lent free of interest, the remainder, £138,000, was part at four per cent., and part at five per cent., the terms being precisely what could have been obtained from any insurance office in the City of London.

The Government, however, agreed to pay half the premiums on policies of insurance for £100,000 on the Maharajah's life (the Maharajah bearing the other half, in respect of which the Government now deduct £1,575 annually from his allowance).

But the additional price exacted for these advances was, that the mansion and all the Suffolk estates, whether bought with the £105,000 (specially provided for the purchase of a family estate), or with the loans raised from Government, or with the Maharajah's own money, shall be sold at the Maharajah's death. Thus the Government have rendered futile the prospect of landed proprietorship for the Maharajah's heirs.

The money result in the year 1884 to the Maharajah of these operations is roughly as follows:—

Annual pension from Government	...	£25,000
Deductions by Government:—		
For interest per annum	... £5,664	
For premiums of insurance	... 1,575	
		7,289

Net sum received by the Maharajah from   _____
      Government per annum.   £17,761

The Maharajah complains that the payments made to him are not in fulfilment of the stipulations of the Treaty. He considers that under the Treaty he ought, after he was of age, to have received the full pension himself paying out the allowances to his relatives and dependants.

If this be correct, the Government have withheld from him sums which, it is calculated, must amount to more than the whole of their advances to him, although the figures of the account have not been furnished by Government.

As to the £105,000 paid him in 1862, if it does, in fact, represent, as he believes, the aggregate amount of sums withheld up to 1859 (calculating his pension at the minimum of four lakhs only), it does not include interest on those accumulations.

It seems hard to the Maharajah, under these circumstances, to be paying large sums of interest every year to the Government, whom he believes to be his debtors; and he hopes, that if ever they should pay him his accumulations, they will pay him back interest on the sums which they have, from time to time, retained, and withheld from his use.

The following is the provision for the widow and children of the Maharajah:—

Value of Suffolk estates (say)	...	...	£200,000
Insurance moneys	...	...	100,000
£72,000 East India Stock	...	...	72,000
			_____
Total provision	...	...	£372,000

This realized at $3\frac{1}{2}$ per cent. would give an income of £13,000, to be divided amongst his widow and children.

We have already stated that the Maharajah contends that the original pension of £45,000 per annum is in its nature *hereditary,* and ought to be continued undiminished after his death to his descendants.

The revenues of the Punjab are not dependent on the tenure of

78

a life, nor do they diminish year by year; and the pension awarded by the Treaty of 1849 should most certainly be regarded as a first charge on those revenues.

From another part of the same book other extracts are supplied, which show how anxious the Maharajah was to have his affairs settled by arbitration.

Extract from work published by the MAHARAJAH, *entitled, "The Maharajah Duleep Singh and the Government."*

How stands the case between the British Government and the Maharajah?

It was thought expedient (it could not be just or right) to annex his kingdom.

To take care of his private estates and property, and to restore them undiminished to him when of age, was the bounden duty of the new Governors of the country, under the circumstances, even had they not been the personal guardians of the boy.

Nevertheless, these estates and property have been appropriated, without apparently a question, or the slightest hesitation on the part of the distinguished and accomplished persons who, from time to time, have constituted the Government of the Punjab, under the new *regime.*

The whole has been treated as if it had been spoil of war.

These estates, as we know, were untouched by the Treaty; but how have we acted towards the Maharajah in our fulfilment of the terms stipulated for by that Treaty?

The Government has explained away all the provisions apparently intended to be secured to the Maharajah, and assured him that, although one clause in it tells him that he is to receive between £40,000 and £50,000 per annum, the next clause, if properly understood, according to official interpretation, entirely takes away such right, and leaves him at the absolute mercy of the Government, to give as much or as little as they please.

Lord Lawrence, in reference to another Indian prince (who was not a British ward), says:—

The question "whether in dealing with an Asiatic ruler, like Shere Ali, the common rules of European international law have any application whatever," is again passed over.

I affirm that it should not so be treated. If international law has no application in this case, then what is the law or principle on which the cause between Shere Ali and ourselves is to be tried. *Are we to be the judges in our own cause?* Are we to decide in accordance with our own interests? Is this an answer which Englishmen will give so grave a matter?

In another place Lord Lawrence justly observes :—

Statesmen should never forget that the real foundations of our power in India do not rest on the interested approval of a noisy few. *They rest on justice*, on the contentment of the millions, who may not always be silent and quiescent, and on their feeling that in spite of the selfish clamour of those who profess to be their guardians and representatives, they may place *implicit trust in the equal justice of our Government*, and in its watchful care of the interests of the masses of the people.

Here we have to do with a treaty and a series of transactions, one party to which is the British Government in its own right, and the other party is the ward of the same British Government.

In the one capacity the British Government want to escape from paying more, or giving up more, than they can help; in the other capacity it has always been their duty, as guardians and trustees, to uphold the interersts of the Maharajah, and claim and recover for him all he could fairly demand, from whomsoever it might be.

The Maharajah accuses the Government of having allowed its attention to the interests of the department to interfere with its duty to his interests, and refuses to satisfied with the correctness of its decision between those interests.

Is it impossible in such a case to provide some impartial tribunal, such as might carry conviction to a reasonable mind that injustice had not been done by irresponsible power? Are there no eminent lawyers of judicial rank whose services might be engaged to hear and decide the conflicting claims?

Or must the nation bear the reproach of its Government, insisting on being judges in its own cause, to the neglect of those sacred principles which Lord Lawrence terms the "foundation of our power in India?"

While the Maharajah was engaged in compiling the book from which the foregoing has been quoted, he had also sent out to India an agent from the firm of Messrs. Farrer & Co., his solicitors, with instructions to examine the records of the Punjab, with a view to establishing the Maharajah's claims on certain private estates.

Shortly after his agent's return, the Maharajah addressed a letter to Lord Kimberley, then Secretary of State of India (March, 1885), forwarding a statement of private estates, claimed by him as inherited from Ranjeet Singh, a Sirdar of the Punjab, and his predecessors, concluding the letter as follows :—

Your Lordship by this time is fully aware that unless the British Government is prepared to accord me speedily some measure of justice, I shall be compelled to abandon permanently my landed estates and position in England, as I am unable adequately to maintain either with the means now accorded to me; in which case, the moderate and legitimate expectations with which I was induced to settle in this country must be utterly disappointed, and I myself and my family be reduced to a state inferior to that of many of the subjects of the State of which I was the Sovereign when my country was annexed by the British Government.

The subjoined statement is the result of a careful inquiry made by the Maharajah's agent in several districts of the Punjab. No estates have been claimed as private property that came into the possession of Ranjeet Singh subsequent to the year 1800, that being the year in which he attained to the sovereignty of the Punjab.

Estates claimed by Duleep Singh as private property (of which some part have been in the possession of his family from the time of Nodh Singh, his great-great-grandfather) :—

In the districts of—

Goojranwala ..61 villages; of which   33 were left by Churrut Singh.

Goojrat ...   10   "   "   6"   "   "   "

Jhelum ...   55   "   "   all   "   "   "
"

(Including the salt-mines of Pind Dadur Khan.)

Sealkote ... 18 villages;   "   9"   "   "   "

81

Goordaspore...6   ”   ”   all   ”   ”
Maha Singh.

Amritsar...   2   ”   left by Nodh Singh.

The remainder of the above were left by Maha Singh, others being acquired by Ranjeet Singh.

The annual value of the above villages is Rs. 204,990- £20,499.

The revenue of the salt mines is now about forty lakhs. (1869.— Rs. 44,91,458=£449,145.) In Sikh times said to be under six lakhs.

The inquiry does not extend all over the Punjab. There are known to be other villages belonging to Churrut Singh, especially about Rawul Pindee.

No reference is here made to the claims of the Maharajah to the intestate estates of deceased relatives, many of whom are known to have died since the date of annexation.

While the question of the Maharajah's claims to private property is under consideration; it may be well to enter here a valuation of the personal property pillaged at Futtehghur during the Mutiny. This return was made out by Sir John Login, and sent in to the Indian Office at the time that compensation claims were called for.

Value of property pillaged at Futtehghur.

	Rupees
Land and houses purchased by His Highness... ...	93,014
Furniture and fittings of all descriptions, including table-furniture, plate, glass, and crockery	74,403
Tent equipage made at Futtehghur...	10,765
Farrash Khana property, consisting of Cashmere tents, carpets, Muslunda quilts, chogas, elephant jhools, &c. ..	20,000
	198,182

In compensation for this claim, the British Government offered £3,000, which the Maharajah refused to accept, considering the proposition an insult.

The Government has never accounted to the Maharajah for the money received for the sale of the house, nor has he received anything

82

in respect of the value of the land, though the papers show that the whole was purchased out of his money, nor any compensation in respect of the contents of the house, which were destroyed at the Mutiny.

Such then is the position of the Maharajah Duleep Singh with the British Government.

For upwards of thirty years has he been at issue with them on various points, small questions no doubt at first, which would have instantly disappeared had the recommendations of Sir John Lawrence and Sir Frederick Currie been adopted; but which, as time went on, became more and more of vital importance to the Maharajah, and, in a corresponding ratio, less and less interesting to the officials who had to deal with the case, as they had no hand in the original Treaty.

Is he, therefore, entirely to blame for his present attitude towards the British nation?

If no excuse can be found for *him,* are the children to suffer for the sins of the father?

Chapter II

DALIP SINGH—THE CRUSADER

Dalip Singh was the youngest son of Maharaja Ranjit Singh. He was born to Maharani Jind Kaur, the youngest queen of the Maharajah on 23rd day of the Bikrami Samvat of *Bhadon* 1895, which falls on 6th September 1838. According to the customs of the times, the *Raj Parohit* Madhu Sudan was asked to prepare the horoscope of the prince. Sohanlal Suri, the author of *Umdat-ut-Twarikh* makes a specific note of the fact, that since it was found in the horoscope of the child that planets Acquarious and Pisces were adversely placed, the detailed horoscope was not prepared by the court astrologer. In the words of Sohanlal Suri, "any intelligent person could easily comprehend the meaning there of. If the Sarkar (Maharaja) would earnestly desire, it would be stated."[1] The prophecy came to be too true in the years to come.

The murder of Maharaja Sher Singh on 15th September 1843 at the hands of his kinsmen Sardars Lehna Singh and Ajit Singh Sandhanwalia and the blood bath that followed for about a week in the streets of Lahore, brought a chance for Dalip Singh getting the throne in somewhat mysterious circumstances. We need not go into the different versions given by the different authorities about the happenings and why Raja Hira Singh, who survived his father Raja Dhyan Singh, who was also a target of the Sandhanwalia Sardars should have picked up this infant child of just five years in preference to the other sons of Ranjit Singh, namely Peshowra Singh and Multana Singh. The blood bath had preceded for nearly one week before Dalip Singh was picked up for the *guddi*. The British-hand in the tragic affairs becomes clear from the secret Despatch by the Governor-General, the Earl of Ellenborough to the Duke of Wellington, then Prime Minister of England, dated 13 August 1843 saying, the affairs of the Punjab will probably receive their denouement from the death of Maharaja Sher

Singh.[2]

Tumultuous Accession and Deposition

By the evening Rajas Dhyan Singh and Suchet Singh and Suchet Singh's commander, Mian Kesari Singh were dead and confusion prevailed around for a week thereafter in the whole of the Khalsa empire. But the situation was worst at the capital city of Lahore with many Sikh regiments in particular, establishing their control in some cantonments for the sake of bargaining with the contenders for the throne as well as the *wazarat*. Dalip Singh was declared Maharaja in this tumultuous situation. He was deposed after a few years in similar circumstances. The British hand is particularly suspected in one way or the other, as they were more or less free from their involvement with Amir Dost Muhammad Khan. A year before the Amir had been restored to the throne of Kabul with his hands and feet tied in the new treaty of peace signed with him and as such the British government were looking for scape-goats within India in a bid to redeem somewhat the loss of prestige they had suffered in the Anglo-Afghan war. For this Sindh Province was first annexed on the plea of bad faith in the war and bad administration. Sindh had a priority as it provided the nearest best seaport for the import of British arms and manufactures for the north-western regions of the country. In Punjab the British would first help create lawlessness and then somehow or the other bring about a clash of arms between the Khalsa army and their own as in the result they were sure the victory would be theirs and the Khalsa would be made to lick their feet for a semblance of a sovereign status. That was the type of blue print already got ready by Lord Hardinge the veteran of many of glorious battles who was to be made the Governor-General of the British Indian empire and Lord Gough as the Commander-in-chief.[3]

The curtain fell on 11 March 1846 when young Dalip Singh was made to sign on dictated lines in the Lahore fort by which the Jammu Kashmir and Ladakh Provinces were annexed and declared a separate sovereign principalty to be handed over to Raja Gulab Singh.The Khalsa army was to be reduced to half or a third of its former strength. Dalip Singh was thus allowed to rule over only a third of the territory of the erstwhile Sikh empire. A British Political Agent was to guide the destinies of the truncated Lahore Kingdom with his headquarters at

Lahore. The Lahore Durbar had thus been made to pay a very high price for its past mistakes and misrule.

The result of the open defiance of British authority in 1847-48 was all the more disastrous. The rebel Sikh forces were again defeated at the battles of Multan, Chillianwala, Ram Nagar and Gujarat—all fought in western Punjab now Pakistan. The next British Governor-General in the person of a young and energetic Lord Dalhousie grabbed this opportunity to strike the last blow to put the Khalsa Raj out of existence. Accordingly, the young Dalip Singh, who was only 11 years of age on 29th March 1849, sat for the last time in the throne chamber in the Palace fort at Lahore to sign the terms of an agreement by which he resigned for himself and his successors all claim to the sovereignty of the Punjab against a paltry amount of Rs. 1,20,000 as his annual pension with permission to retain the title of the Maharaja.[4] This document was personally prepared by the Governor-General on the model of the document on which the Peshwa was made to sign after the defeat of the Maratha Confederacy in 1818 A.D. The annual stipend to Maharaja Dalip Singh was calculated on the same basis as that for the Raja of Satara. Another Rs. 2,80,000 out of Rs. 4 lakhs of maximum allowance allowed in the document, was to be apportioned amongst the widows of Maharaja Ranjit Singh, Kharak Singh, Sher Singh and other ladies of the Palace.[5] He was allowed to retain the title of Maharaja and his ancestral jagirs as well. Then came a challenge in anguish by the people of Punjab for the insults heaped upon them by the British which allowed the Governor-General yet another chance to indict Dalip Singh.

Deportation of Maharaja from Punjab

Lord Dalhousie had himself reached Lahore on 27 November to supervise the arrangements for the Maharaja's removal from amongst his erstwhile subjects and also to receive the priceless *Koh-i-Noor* diamond for the queen of England. Other jewellery and valuables amounting to nearly 16 lakhs of rupees were also confiscated from the *Toshkhana* of the Lahore Durbar.[6] Dr. Login who was in the great confidence of the Governor-General and was appointed a few months earlier as the governor of the Lahore Palace and guardian of the ex-Maharaja, was promoted to the rank of Agent to the Governor-General incharge of Maharaja Dalip Singh. On 27 November itself Lord

Dalhousie held private consultations with Dr. Login for about two hours in the afternoon. As a result of this talk it was also decided to remove from Punjab, Prince Sheo Dev Singh, the only surviving son of Maharaja Sher Singh, who was just a child of six and half years. In view of the great tension then prevailing among the Punjabis on account of the intention of the British to remove the Maharaja and the Prince from amongst them, maximum security precautions were ordered. How much political importance was attached by the Governor-General to the removal of the young Maharaja from the Punjab is evident from the Governor-General's instructions issued from his camp at Bulloke under the signature of foreign secretary, Sir Henry Elliot. The letter says, "The Governor-General having had an opportunity of showing all due respect and courtesy to His Highness at Lahore, conceives that his departure should no longer be delayed," as "it was essential that the Maharaja should not continue to reside in the Punjab after its annexation to the British."

Lord Dalhousie and other British officials who were involved for long in the formulation of the British policy towards Lahore Durbar knew that it would be difficult to have peace in the Punjab so long as the Maharaja, "the symbol of Punjabi nationalism" was there. It was also confirmed in the above letter that Lord Dalhousie had actually wanted to remove the Maharaja from the Punjab soon after annexation but this had to be postponed for a number of reasons, one of which was "the hot weather ahead." The letter further impressed on Dr. Login that even after the arrival of the Maharaja at Fatehgarh, he should continue to take fullest security precautions in view of the possibility of efforts to rescue Dalip Singh. It was also hinted that Maharani Jindan's "avowed intention was to regain possession of her son, the Maharaja."

The letter also made it clear that the British were not even prepared to take the risk of allowing any male issue of the Lahore royal family to remain in the Punjab for the reason that it should not be possible for anybody to start any movement in the name of any such male member at any future date. Therefore, the orders about the removal of Prince Sheo Dev Singh simultaneously with Maharaja Dalip Singh. It was stated, that "The Governor-General conceives it to be desirable to remove at the same time from the Punjab the child who is, it is believed, the only legitimate son of the late Maharajah Sher Singh.

He can for the present occupy the same residence as the Maharajah, under such regulations as may be thought right." The letter further cautioned Dr. Login that, "in both cases, a very careful selection should be made of the attendants who are to accompany them and both should be prevented from having anyone about them, except such persons as Dr. Login may consider from his experience to be worthy of trust."

Major H.P. Burn, Deputy Secretary of the Punjab Board of Administration, while forwarding the above letter of Sir Elliot to Dr. Login further stated, by directions of the Board, that while on march, "no man of doubtful character should be permitted to accompany the camp of the Maharaja; that in addition to the armed guard, two or three trusted persons should at all times remain with the Maharaja in order to prevent his being inveigled away at night, quite as much as against armed violence."

The only change made in the programme already settled was to allow the mother and the maternal uncle of Prince Sheo Dev Singh to accompany him to Fatehgarh and to live with him there for some years till the child had sufficiently grown up. This was done on the advice of Dr. Login himself. The Governor-General almost followed the Maharaja's party till its arrival at Fatehgarh on 21 February 1850.

Weaning Away of Dalip Singh from his Heritage and Culture

It was at Fatehgarh that Dr. Login used every artful device to wean away the young Maharaja, not only from his own people, but also his own culture and heritage in accordance with a set programme, though outwardly and even in the public despatches exchanged between him and the Governor-General, it was maintained that the young Maharaja was allowed complete freedom of action and thought but it was a farce.

It may be stated in this connection that Dalip Singh was neither so young nor so immature as to have remained either ignorant of or unconcerned about the great unheavals through which he and his government had passed during the last few years.

According to the testimony of Dr. Login himself, "Dalip Singh was much above the average in intelligence, that he knew Persian and vernacular very well and was attempting to learn painting." Unlike most of the princes of his age, Dalip Singh had never even tasted wine so far,

88

reported Dr. Login. Therefore, with an intelligent boy like him the British had to use very subtle methods to detract his mind from his past and to make him appreciate the English character and culture.

The first thing done by Dr. Login on arriving at Fatehgarh, therefore, was to dispense with a number of personal servants of the Maharaja and place in their stead persons of his confidence around him, these persons were previously in Dr. Login's employ at Lucknow for a similar job with the young Nawab of Oudh. Dr. Login was actually keen to win over the Maharaja to the western culture before he would attain maturity. He confided to his wife in England, *vide* his letter to her dated, 6 March 1850. He wrote, "I shall be glad when you join me, for I can expect to have more than two or three years in which we can influence the young Maharajah's mind favourably towards our domestic life and I must not lose them on any account." Further hinting at the political significance of his mission, Dr. Login therefore exhorted her "to join him, as early as possible, in this task even though it meant running a little risk to her health, so as to occupy a position of so much usefulness, towards one who may yet influence so many thousands of people."

Actually it did not take the Logins or the Governor-General long to succeed in their mission of missions. Within a few months of his residence at Fatehgarh it was given out that the young Maharaja, of his own free will, was not desirous of marrying the sister of Raja Sher Singh of Attari with whom he was betrothed long back.[7] Lord Dalhousie's comments on receiving information about so great a change in the Maharaja in so short a time is worth noting. He wrote back, "I should object decidedly, and do not wish to countenance any relations henceforth between the Maharaja and the Sikhs, either by alliance with a Sikh family, or sympathy with a Sikh feeling."

Soon after by December 1850 Dr. Login was happy to report to the Governor-General, that the Maharaja had expressed a desire to be converted to Christianity of his own free will.[8] All this alleged change in Maharaja's mind was the result, claimed Dr. Login, because the only instruction which the young Maharaja was allowed by his own people was about religious matters formed of fables of old Hindu mythology which were self contradictory, and that a copy of *Granth Sahib* he had asked for the Maharaja, while leaving Lahore, was not complied with.

89

In fact, as is evident from the foregoing paras, it was hardly the aim of the British authorities that Dalip Singh should learn the Sikh scriptures. That also becomes clear from the fact that when Prince Sheo Dev Singh's mother objected to her son being given the same instructions by English knowing tutors as were given to Maharaja Dalip Singh, Dr. Login immediately decided to separate Dalip Singh from what, he described, "such influences of the *shahzada* and her mother" and sent Shiv Deo Singh and his mother to live at Dehra Dun.

At one stage the Logins expressed their uneasiness about the fact that Maharaja still continued to have craving for the Punjabi dishes. Therefore as soon as he started showing inclination to western type of food, this fact was given wide publicity among the official and private British circles.

Soon after Dr. Login explained that, "the Maharaja discarded his personal tastes and finally his religion. So much so that, he even wished to get his hair cut and started showing an eagerness to be converted to Christian religion."[9]

On getting that report from Dr. Login, Lord Dalhousie wrote back a personal letter on 15 February 1853 to the Maharaja, appreciating his conduct with the remarks that, "by doing that the Maharaja will set to his countrymen in India, an example of a pure and blameless life such as is befitting a Christian."[10] Dalhousie however advised Dr. Login that the Maharaja's name should not be changed and that his baptism should be performed at his residence without giving "notoriety" to the event. It had already been decided, for obvious political considerations, that the conversion of the Maharaja should take place before he was sent to England which was also then under the active consideration of the authorities. The Maharaja was, therefore, converted on 8 March 1853 as per instructions, and to the great rejoicing of the Governor-General, Dr. Login, Henry Lawrence and others, who were eagerly awaiting for this event to happen.[11] Writing to Login after the Maharaja's formal conversion, Lord Dalhousie stated, "I rejoice deeply and sincerely in this good issue to the great change the boy had passed through. I regard it as a very remarkable event in history and in every way gratifying."[12]

Maharaja Sent to England

This having been done, the Maharaja was made to sail to England on 19 April 1854, just a few months before he was to attain the age of maturity. As a parting gift the Governor-General presented to him a copy of the Bible, which he described "as the best of all gifts, since, in it alone is to be found the secret of real happiness either in this world or in that which is to come." Rani Dukhne, the mother of Prince Sheo Dev Singh, however, succeeded, though to the great displeasure of the British, in maintaining intact the religion of her young son. Partly from this consideration the British also agreed to her prayer not to send Sheo Dev Singh to England with Dalip Singh, but the Shahzada was to reside away from the Punjab.[13]

Maharaja Dalip Singh's Image in the Eyes of the Sikhs

The most significant thing to be noted was that inspite of all the steps taken by the British to deprive the Sikhs of even the distant possibility of reviving their freedom struggle in the names of any of the scions of their erstwhile rulers the Sikhs and in particular all Punjabi nationalists continued to cherish the memory of this unfortunate Maharaja who had become a hero in their eyes. This fact continued to worry the British authorities till Dalip Singh had not died and as is well known he died as a rebel against the British. A few instances covering the first decade of his exile may prove this fact. While the Maharaja was being taken to Mussourie during the summer of 1852, he had expressed a desire to visit Haridwar for a sacred bath. This was the period when a large number of pilgrims from the Punjab had gathered at Haridwar for a dip in the sacred river on the occasion of Baisakhi festival. The British authorities were afraid that if the people at Haridwar came to know about their ex-Maharaja's presence there they would surely try to have a glimpse of him, if nothing more.

Therefore in order to decoy the multitude, the British authorities cleverly sent the Maharaja's carriage and escort, to one direction of the river, while the Maharaja was taken to another, but this did not work, because a large number of Punjabis succeeded in reaching near the elephant on which Dalip Singh was returning from the river side. They surrounded the elephant and "gave tumultuous ovation" to their dear Maharaja.

Similarly inspite of all precautions taken to keep the departure of the Maharaja to England as guarded a secret as possible the news was soon out. What it caused to the Punjabis, is reflected in a short poem written by Munshi Ghulam Sarwar and published in the issue of *Koh-i-Noor* the same year. The poem is entitled "Wailings of the Punjabis on the Departure of their Maharaja."

Again in March 1861 when Maharaja Dalip Singh had arrived in Calcutta from England to fetch his mother as decided by the British and was staying at the Spencers Hotel awaiting the arrival of his mother there from Nepal, at that time some Sikh Regiments were returning from the China war. As soon as they came to know that Maharaja Dalip Singh was staying there, they moved to his hotel in a body and offered to him a tumultuous ovation. This made the then Governor-General so much unnerved that he cancelled the up country tour of the Maharaja as planned earlier and sent him back to England by first available ship alongwith Maharani Jindan.

Causes of Rift with the British

The causes which brought about an open rift between Dalip Singh and the British were both personal and political.

On the personal level the Maharaja was sore on a number of issues. He felt agitated at the British refusal to allow him to settle in India. He was equally unhappy over the arbitrary decrease in his pension. He also claimed a right to his ancestral property in the Punjab, which according to him, had not been alienated by the agreement of March 29, 1849.[14] According to him the famous gem *Koh-i-Noor* too was a part of his personal jewellery and not the State property.[15]

In a letter published in *"The Times"* issue of August 31, 1882, Dalip Singh gave vent to his personal grievances in London. He wrote that he was unjustly deprived of his kingdom yielding an annual revenue of 250,000, for a life-stipend of merely 25,000 per annum, which after deduction of certain charges did not exceed 13,000 per year. The letter ends with the words, "What chance have I of obtaining justice, considering that my despoiler, guardian, judge, advocate and jury is the British nation itself."[16] In fact a good part of the change in the mind of Maharaja Dalip Singh had been due to his mother's telling him how and what they had lost at the hands of the British.

It seemed that Dalip Singh had been intentionally avoiding doing any thing to show to his guardians, the Logins, in respect of his personal privileges till he had reached the age of 16 years. There could be no doubt that Fakir Nurruddin, Maharaja Ranjit Singh's most trusted Minister-in-charge of the Palace and then personal tutor of young Dalip Singh must have also dinned such ideas into his ears, before the Logins actually got rid of him and other members of his personal staff in 1853. Therefore his not creating any fuss about his conversion to Christian faith and for the sake of satisfying the whims of Logins quietly agreed to be separated from his cousin Shiv Deo Singh.

Yet the manner Dalip Singh came out in his true self claiming his personal jagirs and pension as agreed to by the British in the so-called *ahadnama* or treaty of abdication as sovereign of Punjab, should not keep any one in doubt that the Prince was neither that innocent nor that naive while dealing with his imperial guardians. If that was so then it would not be logical to believe that a single lecture from a British Labour M.P. John Bright[17] which Dalip Singh is said to have heard or read about in 1859 while on his Continental tour arranged for him by the British[17] simply to win him over all the more to the European way of life, could have been the only turning point in his career, though the lecture would have certainly set the sensitive mind of young Maharaja to ponder over the issue more seriously. Coincidentally the British authorities had also then arranged a few meetings between Dalip Singh and a young daughter of the deported Raja of Cochin so as to get the two Indian deprived royal families made Christian to join in wedlock. But the outright refusal by Dalip Singh to marry that princess saying that marriage was his personal affair was enough to show how his mind was working.

About Maharani Jindan's role, Lady Login and the British intelligence reports admit that Maharani Jindan before her death in 1864 had instilled in her son's heart strong patriotic feelings and that he was determined to go to India even if he might have to go through Russia. The question is why Dalip Singh should have thought of slipping in to Russia in particular or to India through Russia. The reason was that soon after Dalip Singh was made aware about the strong rumours then afloat in the Punjab about the prophecies made by Guru Gobind Singh about his returning to Punjab as the Maharaja with perhaps Russian help, the Kukas had particulary pinned their faith in the return of Dalip.

Singh to power as prophesied in a number of "Sakhis". One Sakhi then current in the Punjab was that "Dalip Singh will come to Punjab and rising from the west the Khalsa will predominate in the east."[18]

According to another "Sakhi" Kuka Bishan Singh was destined to lead a Muhammadan army of liberation in the Punjab through the north-western frontiers of India. Bishan Singh Arora alluded to in this "Sakhi" was a wealthy merchant of Kabul with business centres in Bukhara, Russia and Peshawar. Therefore simultaneously with Gurcharan Singh Kuka, Bishan Singh was also attempting an alliance with the Russian governor of Bokhara for the liberation of the Punjab.

Curiously enough, not only the Sikhs, but some Indian rulers had also been attempting to obtain Russian help against the British. In 1862 the ruler of Indore and in 1868 the Maharaja of Jammu and Kashmir are supposed to have sent their emissaries to the Governor of Tashkend for enlisting his support in their favour. The Maharaja of Jammu and Kashmir had even raised a "Kuka" Regiment in his forces.[19]

Dalip Singh was certainly not unaware about these developments in India when he applied for permission to visit the Punjab for the ostensible purpose of collecting necessary information about his ancestral jagirs. The British official circles in India were not prepared to believe that it was the only reason of Dalip Singh's visit to the country. They therefore recommended that Maharaja should not be allowed to enter the country.

Writing on the subject, the then Lt. Governor of the Punjab informed the Viceroy, Marquis of Ripon that "No doubt the Maharaja's conversion to Christianity and his long residence in England have created a wide gulf between him and the people of his country, but we must not give too much weight to that. There are thousands of Sikhs, who look for the restoration of the Khalsa some day or other; and at present there is a wide-spread movement going on among the Kukas, which though not in itself dangerous might easily become so, on the arrival of Dalip Singh, the injured representative of the Lahore family."[20]

Bengali Nationalists and Dalip Singh

Even the news about the intending visit of Dalip Singh to India was sufficient to catch the imagination of many of the nationalists in

94

the country. The nationalist forces in Bengal considered it as a fit opportunity to inspire the Punjabis against the British. They therefore circulated a large number of secret pamphlets in the various cities and towns of the Punjab with the appeal that all should rally under the banner of the Maharaja Dalip Singh. The pamphlets bore the slogan *"Maharaja Dalip Singh Ki Jai."*[21] There was a strong reason for the Bengali nationalists to take up the cause of Dalip Singh as a hero of the anti-British movement. Bengalis had to a great extent been the leading figures in the Punjab education service and also in the medical profession and the Punjabi people had shown them great respect. Sardar Dayal Singh Majithia who had become a great pioneering figure in the field of education and social reform in Punjab had built up a strong base in Bengal where his family members were imprisoned by the British after annexation.

Sardar Dayal Singh Majithia having been influenced greatly by the Brahmo Samaj movement in Bengal had set up at Lahore a nationalist English daily the *Tribune* besides the Dayal Singh College and Library under a Trust. This is what the *Tribune* in its issue of August, 1883 wrote editorially: "It is true that the Maharaja has been in England since a long time and has adopted English manners, customs and modes of life, but yet he could not have forgotten that he was born in this country and that he is the son of one of the most powerful of Indian Princes. Brilliant associations crowd round his infancy which all his education and foreign training may not have been able altogether to efface, and it is, therefore, natural that he should feel a longing to see the land with which those associations are so intimately connected. Amidst all the gaieties of Elveden Hall and the pleasures of an English-married life, it was impossible for him to forget that he was by birth a native of India. And that we think is reason enough to impel him to visit the country of his forefathers."

There was already enough of tension in the country caused by the vernacular Press Act, the Arms Act of 1878, the Ilbert Bill controversy and the second Anglo-Afghan War. The British government did not want to add to their troubles by allowing Dalip Singh to visit India at that time. His request was, therefore, turned down and instead the government allowed S. Thakur Singh Sandhanwalia, Dalip Singh's first cousin, to contact the Maharaja in England and post him with the facts about his jagirs, if any. Thakur Singh was in a way glad to get this opportunity. He was equally disgruntled against the British in view of their having placed his jagirs under the Court of Ward. Whatever may be the views of the higher authorities, local officials themselves admitted that Thakur Singh was decidedly "a man of some light and leading among the Sikhs." During his nearly one year of stay in England Thakur Singh played a significant role in preparing Dalip Singh for a struggle with the British. Plans were also prepared for establishing Dalip Singh's contacts with the people and princes of the Punjab. Thakur Singh's personal servants and adherents namely Jawahar Singh, Sohan Lal, Anup Singh, Banarasi Dass Kuka and Arur Singh alias Partap Singh played a very conspicuous role in this connection during the next few years.[22]

The political situation in Europe and the middle East was no less favourable for Indian nationalists. The Irish nationalists were already sympathetically disposed towards Dalip Singh and an Irish Fanian, a retired Major from the British army, had joined him for the purpose.[23] France and Germany were engaged in fomenting troubles against the British in Egypt and Turkey through the Islamite League and the Wahabis. In India too, upper class Muhammadans had come under the influence of these movements. The cities of Bombay, Bhopal, Lucknow, Patna, Calcutta, Hyderabad Deccan were among their strongholds. The movement had the backing of influential people like the Begum of Bhopal and her husband Nawab Sadiq Hussain, Hasan Ali, a cousin of Budr-ud-Din Tayabji then living in Constantinople, Maulvi Rehmat Ullah of Delhi who had escaped to Arabia during the 1857, the rebellious Sheikh Ahmed of (Alippo) and Abdul Rasul Kashmiri to mention only a few names. Abdul Rasul and one Sheikh Jamal-ul-Din, the latter variously described as an Afghan or a Persian, had been propagating against the British not only in India and the middle East but in England and France as well. Later both of them had actively supported Dalip Singh in Russia, when the Maharaja had managed to reach Mascow.[24]

The Maharaja Forms a National Government of India

It was in these circumstances that Dalip Singh decided to make a bid. He gave up his English citizenship and set up his headquarters in Paris from where on 10th January, 1886, he announced the

96

establishment of an independent *emigre* government at Pondicherry with Sardar Thakur Singh as his Prime Minister. By then Thakur Singh had taken up his residence in Pondicherry and established secret liaison with a number of Sikh regiments serving under the British. The rulers of Chamba, Faridkot, Nabha and Kishan Kaur, the Dowager Rani of Ballabgarh whose son Nahar Singh was hanged by the British in the 1857 rebellion, had already promised support.

Support of the nationalist Bengalis was assured by one Shashi Bhushan Mukherji then in exile in Pondicherry and running a paper *The Beaver* and Kumar Indra Chander Singh of Calcutta. In Hyderabad Deccan, Raja Narinder Prakash, a member of the late Raja Chandu Lal's family and the Nawab's Peshkaar, was in constant touch with Thakur Singh, while almost all the Sikhs in Hyderabad Deccan had pledged to support their Maharaja at the crucial stage. Banarasi Dass, another Kuka revolutionary, went to Nepal for the same purpose.[25]

It was planned that at the time of Dalip Singh's coming to India with Russian support, the entire population of Punjab would rise and destroy means of communication and transportation in the rear of the British force. The Sikh soldiers in the British army would also join him, while the Indian soldiers in the service of the Princes would refuse to fight for the British. After the defeat of the British, Dalip Singh intended to establish a government representing all communities and interests in co-operation with the Indian Princes.

The Proclamation of 1886

This plan was spelt out in a secret proclamation issued by the Maharaja from Paris on 7th February 1886. The proclamation opens with the remarks: "Courage! Countrymen, Courage! We, your flesh and blood, tell you, lift up your bowed-down heads and by the help of the Almighty Aryavarta shall once more be free and the 'Rising Young India' shall enjoy both liberty and self-government". He exhorted his countrymen to share with him, "the glory of liberating the mother country." To the Sikhs he asked, "prepare for the advent of their lawful, sovereign" and to learn from the "Sakhis" their "glorious destiny predicted by *Dusswan Padshah*".[26] He also addressed secret letters to the Maharaja of Jammu and Kashmir and other Punjab chiefs and princes.

Having issued the above proclamation from Paris, Dalip Singh reached Moscow from where he sent through Arur Singh two separate letters one to the Raja of Indore and the other to the deposed King of Oudh. Arur Singh was also the bearer of one general appeal to all other Indian princes. To the ex-king of Oudh, Dalip Singh wrote, "With great joy I announce to you that I have reached Russia, and hope through the mercy of god and with the aid of the Emperor of the Russia soon to come to India and deliver Your Majesty from the hands of the accursed English and replace you on your throne." Dalip Singh asked all the princes to send assurances to the Czar of Russia with whose aid "he was expected to deliver them from bondage."

Dalip Singh's venture created so much enthusiasm in the Punjab that a local paper *Dhumketu* published the following verses eulogising him : **"oh! wicked English men, do you remember the insults which you have heaped on the lion (Dalip Singh); a lion about to make a trial of strength with another lion (British); China, Burma and Japan are free, why shall he (Dalip Singh) suffer so much agony; from a distance and with a fire of hope burning in his heart, he is roaring out, awake ye Sikhs, quit your beds and awake; have ye forgotten your days of prosperity when this earth with its sky and mountain shook under your feet; have you forgotten the bright jewel Koh-i-Noor; where is that diamond gone; to live in bondage is to live in hell; chop off the cruel fetters of bondage."[27]**

In Moscow one Jamal-ud-Din introduced the Maharaja to the Russian officials, including Kot Koff, an official in the Russian army. Kot Koff commended Dalip Singh's plan and promised him the support of the Russian army. Abdul Rasul acted as his secretary and introduced him to the local Muslims.[28]

Seeks Alliance with the Czar of Russia

Thus assured of success Dalip Singh addressed a lengthy letter to the Emperor of Russia in which he particularly drew the Czar's attention to the benefits which will accrue to the economy of Russia as a result of the liberation of India from the British yoke. The upright and business like tone of the letter speaks volumes about the Maharaja's mature understanding of the political game so necessary for the success of an alliance with Russia. In the memorial addressed to the Czar Dalip

98

Singh stated :

"Before proceeding to lay before the Imperial government the humble prayer of the Princes and the people of India for deliverance from their oppressors, I think it necessary to state here that for myself I seek no gain whatsoever, for I am a patriot and only seek to deliver some 2,50,00,000 of my countrymen from the cruel yoke of the British rulers and to benefit the deliverer at the same time and will serve the Imperial government (should it think proper to employ me) without any remuneration whatsoever." Commenting on the political relationship between India and Russia after the former's deliverance from the British yoke, Dalip Singh wrote that "the princes of India when free and if allowed to manage their affairs in their own way, would join together and pay a large tribute annually into the Russian Treasury. Although I am authorised to name only 30 lakhs per annum yet in my opinion after the settling down of the country they could easily pay between 80 lakhs and a crore." As to the economic benefits to Russia, Dalip Singh gave a complete picture of what the British were gaining. He informed the Czar that the British raised an annual revenue from the country of some 5 crore to 6 crore sterling. Out of which an army of 10 lakhs European and officers and English civilians (who receive very high salaries) about atleast 25,000 and the rest is employed in the administration of the country, and in the payment of interest upon capital advanced by England for the construction of rail, road and upon the Public debt of India and pensions to retired officials in England. Also the import and export trade between England and India amounting to some 500 lakhs per annum each way would be secured to Russia. India is indeed a gold mine to England and most of her wealth has been and is derived from that source. I have been much struck already during my very short stay in Russia with the low value of things in this country for want (in my opinion) of suitable markets for their disposal. But could the same commodities be taken to India, I feel persuaded that from 100 to 500 per cent over the prices they fetch here would be realized for them there. The markets of central Asian countries are not to be compared with that of India".

At the end, Dalip Singh also drew the attention of the Czar to the prophecy made in the "Sakhis" for his regaining the sovereignty of the

Punjab with the assistance of a foreign power and claimed that if 200,000 Russian soldiers and 2,000 cannon were placed at his disposal, he was sure to be supported by nearly 300,000 soldiers in the forces of the Indian princes, 45,000 Sikh soldiers in the British Indian army and the entire Sikh population of the Punjab numbering 800,000."

Failure of the Mission

Inspite of his stay in Russia for over 18 months and all his efforts the Maharaja failed to get any favourable response from the government of Russia. He even failed to get an interview with the Czar or get any financial support inspite of the occasional attempts by certain sections to boost up his case. One such example was an article published in his favour in the Moscow Gazette of 15-17 September 1887. The article gave a long account of how Dalip Singh was cheated out of his kingdom and stated, "we welcome him with the conviction that he will find among us all the sympathy which his fate demands".[29]

There were many reasons for the failure of Dalip Singh's mission. Firstly, Kot Koff, on whose personal influence the Maharaja depended so much, died soon after. Secondly, the Foreign Minister of the Czar was not in favour of such a venture on account of the failure of the Russian Policy in Bulgaria and Afghanistan.[29] Thirdly, Dalip Singh was wrong in his presumption that the Indian rulers would be able to help him materially. He was certainly wrong to think that of any person, the Maharaja of Jammu and Kashmir, whose State once formed a part of the Lahore kingdom, would be his active ally against the British inspite of the fact that the latter was not very happy with the British. Also Dalip Singh's last letter to the Maharaja of Jammu and Kashmir clearly betrayed the former's bitterness against the latter. "I was young when the English took me away from my country," wrote Dalip Singh, "and the administration was left in the hands of your ancestors. They did not look to my interests and ruined the State. This was not a loyal act, but I have forgiven the past. For the future, I command that whatever S. Thakur Singh thinks, is best for myself and you and should be carried out. So shall the stain on your name be removed; otherwise no such opportunity will again occur." How could the ruler of Jammu and Kashmir own all this blame? Lastly, S. Thakur Singh's death in Pondicherry and later Arur Singh's arrest at Calcutta on the 5th August,

1887 altogether changed the position in India.[30] Aru
to the detection of almost all the agents of Dalip Si

Abdul Rasul's Mission

Having been disappointed with the Indian rule
government, Dalip Singh attempted to get support fro
opposed to the British. For this purpose he depute
France, Germany, Austria and Turkey. None of the European countries,
however, responded to his call on the plea that the Maharaja had no
active support in India. It was only in Turkey that anti-British party led
by Zobair Pasha, the ex-Prime Minister of Sudan and Ahmad Mukhtar
Pasha, a Minister of the Turkish government, assured Abdul Rasul of
their active support to Dalip Singh. Their plea was to close the Suez
canal as soon as there was a rising in the Punjab, Sikandar Khan of
Herat and Alikhanoff, the governor of Panjdeh, had also shown interest
in the plan.[32]

But before Abdul Rasul could finalize the plan and contact the
Maharaja in Moscow, Dalip Singh left for Keiff in April, 1888 and from
there he reached Paris on November 3 the same year, a dejected and
disappointed soul.[33]

The only interesting part of this episode is that even after Dalip
Singh had left Moscow parties of innocent Punjabis were detected
tracking their way to Russia in the vain hope that what was written in
the "Sakhis" must come true. These included a party of Kukas from
Amritsar district consisting of Maha Singh, Sawal Singh and Wadu
Singh. They had travelled *via* Dera Ismail Khan and Gilgit to reach
Tashkend in search of their "lost Maharaja". Another group consisting
of Babas Sunder Singh, Indar Singh and Badri from Jullundhar were
detected at Mashed. Moti, a 40-year old Muslim *jheor* from Gurdaspur,
even committed suicide when detected at Mashed on his way to Russia
for the same purpose.

It could however be concluded that though Maharaja Dalip Singh
had failed in his historic role of making his motherland free from the
British yoke, yet the manner he had attempted to achieve his objective
and the persistence and perseverance shown by him inspite of many
odds he faced speaks volumes about his valour and his political
sagacity. This was true inspite of the fact that the future commentators

d to read too much in his so-called death testament about his ...ntance to have abandoned the allegiance to the British Crown. That ...as nothing but the expression of an agonized soul searching for an answer as to where he had gone wrong and why? It was also admitting of the fact though late, that India with her orthodox thinking and the out of date Princely order had to have completely recast her options before she could again become a sovereign nation and a free country. Dalip Singh had perhaps taken up the mission much too early for the country. But the way he did it and with great self pride as a son of India speaks volumes. He gave us the slogans like "Young India" and "Arya Varat". He was the first from the Princely order to have proved by giving figures how India was the real strength behind the economic and military power of the British. Was he not the forerunner of Rash Behari and Subhash Bose and many other Indian patriots who thought that an armed intervention through a country opposed to the British could only deliver Hindustan from their yoke?

The Real Dalip Singh

Dalip Singh breathed his last on 22 October 1893 at the age of 55 years. In the obituary published in *The Tribune* issue of 25th October, the paper mournfully recalling the principal traits of the Maharaja's character concluded, "We have heard from the Punjabi gentlemen who had seen him in England that he had forgotten nothing of his life at Lahore. He loved to talk of his old days, and his eyes were filled with tears, as he spoke of his old playmates, his *tahlias* (personal attendants), his favourite horses and the georgeously uniformed regiment of infants consisting of the cadets coming of the noblest houses in the Punjab."[34]

That was in fact the real Dalip Singh, the ex-Maharaja of the last of the sovereign States of India.

—**M.L. Ahluwalia**

References

1. *Umdat-ut-Twarikh,* Daftar III, Prt-V English translation by Shri V.S. Suri, 1961, edition p. 525.
2. Sohan Lal Suri *op. cit.,* Daftar IV, pp. 26-27. Colchestor, Life of Earl of Ellenborough, p. 367. *See* also Sita Ram: Sunset of the Sikh Empire, pp. 63-64.

3. Things moved rather quickly for the British in view of the unchecked lawlessness which prevailed in the Kingdom between 1843-1845. The Khalsa army was led into the well.

4. By M.L. Ahluwalia, entitled "Some Facts Behind the Sikh Revolt of 1847-48," I.H.R.C. Progs. Vols Nos. XXXV, XXXVI & XXXVII, Part II. Also Lord Dalhousie's *letters* to John Hob House, President of the Board of Control in London, dated 24 March, and 4th April, 1849. For text of abdication, *See* Maharaja Dhuleep Singh's Correspondence, Vol. III Appendix XV-Editor Dr. Ganda Singh. pp. 647-75, Punjabi University, Patiala.

5. Broughton Papers.

6. The Maharaja was also allowed to retain his personal jewellery worth rupees one lakh. Governor-General's Despatch to Secret Committee of 1849, No. 59.

7. Life of Sir Login, by Lady Login pp. 212-13 and 220.

8. Sec. Cons. Nos. 83-99, dt. 28 February 1851 and Nos. 70-72, dated 28 March 1851.

9. Sec. Cons. dated 28th March 1851 No. 72.

10. Life of Sir Login *op. cit.* p. 34.

11. The Court of Directors' consent for the deportation of the Maharaja to England was received in January 1854. Login's *op. cit.* p. 318.

12. *Ibid,* p. 307.

13. In 1860, Shahzada Sheo Dev Singh proposed to marry the daughter of the Sardar of Sham Gurh much to the dislike of the British.

14. Treaties, Engagements & Sanads of India, Vol. No. VIII, 4th Ed. 1899. pp. 170-71 No. IXIV; Maharajah Duleep Singh's Government A Narrative, London, 1884, Foreign Deptt. Secret, I progs of Dec. 1883 Nos. 10-11.

15. Lady Login's Recollections, by E. Dalhousie Login, 123-24.

16. Annexation of the Punjab and the Maharaja Duleep Singh, by E. Bell, Appendix B. 92-96.

17. John Bright was speaking on the subject "Wrongs of the Unhappy Natives under British Domination". See Lady Login's Recollections, pp. 180-207.

18. For. Deptt. Sec. I Progs. May 1883, Nos. 8, 11 & 59.

19. For. Deptt. Sec. I Progs. Aug. 1889, Nos. 114-15.

20. For. Deptt. Sec. I Progs. December 1883, Nos. 8-17.

21. For. Deptt. Sec. I Progs. December 1883, Nos. 8-17.

22. For. Deptt. Sec. I Progs. Aug. 1887, Nos. 15-51 (K.W.)

23. For. Deptt. Sec. I Progs. Oct. 1887, No. 90 and Nov. 1887, Nos. I-30.

24. For. Deptt. Sec. I Progs. May 1888, Nos. 40-41.

25. For. Deptt. Sec. I Progs. Oct. 1887, No. 90 and Nov. 1887, Nos. 1-30.

26. For. Sec. Progs. May, 1886, No. 41.

27. *Op. cit.* For. Sec. Progs. May, 1888, Nos. 41-41.

28. For. Deptt. Sec. I Progs. Jan., 1886, No. 9.

29. For. Deptt. Sec. Aug. 1888 Nos. 13-14.

30. For. Deptt. Sec. I Progs. Nov. 1887, No. 2.

31. For. Deptt. Sec. I Progs. Aug. 1887, No. 14.

32. For. Deptt. Sec. I Progs. No. 15-16.

33. For. Deptt. Sec. I Progs. Apr. 1889, Nos. 41-45.

34. The regiment was named as *"Vanar Sena"* of Lord Hanuman and *"Dashmesh Sena"* of Guru Gobind Singh.

Chapter III

MAHARAJA DALIP SINGH'S VISIT TO RUSSIA AS VIEWED BY BRITISH GOVERNMENT
(BASED ON PRIVATE LETTERS)

This paper is based on private letters of Lord Cross, more than two dozen in number. During my researches in the old India Office Library London in 1964, I came across the private letters of Richard Assheton Cross 1st Viscount (1823-1914). Lord Cross has been stated to be the "greatest home secretary" of the 19th century of England. Lord Dissraeli brought Cross into his cabinet as Home Secretary. He was appointed the Secretary of State for India in 1886 and he held this office from 1886-1892.

The letters were written *by* Lord Cross, the Secretary of State for India to Lord Dufferin, the Governor General of India. These letters cover the period from August 6, 1886 to December 25th, 1887. The years 1886 and 1887 are very significant in the life of Maharaja Dalip Singh. He returned disappointed from Aden as he was not allowed to enter India. He, therefore, reached a hotel in Paris by April, 1886. How he went to Russia in disguise and how he was pursued by the agent of British Government, how his personal attendant, Watson, supplied day to day information regarding his master to the Secretary of State, (to the British Government) etc. are the aspects on which these letters throw light. Since these letters were personal and private they give the real mind of Lord Cross about Maharaja Dalip Singh and his activities.

As Home Secretary Sir Richard had known the importance of Intelligence Department. In his letters to Lord Dufferin he advised him to reorganise the Intelligence Department specially to keep a strict watch on Maharaja Dalip Singh. He wrote on January 6, 1887, "I hope you are getting on with your improved Intelligence Department of Police."[1] Again he wrote on February 3, 1887, "I also telegraphed to you the last news which we have heard of Dhuleep Singh through Sir R. Montgomery. Copies of the papers go to you by this mail. All this, however, makes me very anxious that your Intelligence Department should be improved and thoroughly organised ...".[2] He stressed this point in another letter dated March 25th 1887, "you are quite right in taking steps to insure that Intelligence Department is reorganised on a proper basis but it is very necessary especially now that we have a row for in Dhuleep Singh".[3]

After embracing Sikhism at Aden Maharaja Dalip Singh wrote a letter to "Times of India". He stated therein, "Although the Indian Government succeeded in preventing me from reaching Bombay lately. Yet they are not able to close all the roads that there are to India, for when I return I can either land at Goa or Pondicherry, or if I fancy an overland route where I can enter the Punjab through Russia."

This greatly perturbed the Secretary of State and he wrote to Lord Dufferin on the 8th Sept. 1886, "what has been the effect of Dhuleep Singh's manifesto? I am all for reducing any real and genuine grievances and that without delay."[4] Again he asserted in a letter, "whatever might have been done with Dhuleep Singh in past times, it is impossible to treat with him now. He has openly joined his former religion. He has issued treasonable proclamation. He would enter into no terms. He will not forgive his imprisonment at Aden. All we can do is to watch and guard against him. We keep through F.O.(Foreign Officer) the strictest watch upon his movements in Paris. As we are informed, he is to leave in company with a young girl for Constantinople this morning. You shall be informed by telegraph of all that we can learn. Meanwhile look after his friend in relations in Pondicherry."[5]

The Secretary of State appears to have appointed deGiers to follow the activities of Maharaja Dalip Singh. Maharaja Dalip Singh's old servant named Watson was tipped to report to the Secretary of State. Watson wrote several letters to Lord Cross which were forwarded to Lord Dufferin in original as the former writes, "I have sent you some letters from Dhuleep Singh's old servant Watson. Are you still of the same opinion as to the Maharaja's lack of power for evil"?[6]

Men to Watch

Thakur Singh Sindhanwalia of Rajasansi, district Amritsar was a cousin of Maharaja Dalip Singh. He was successful in persuading him to rejoin the faith of his forefathers during his visit to England in 1885.[7] He was considered the arch enemy of the British Government and he had therefore fled with his family to Pondicherry, a French settlement in India. But Thakur Singh continued to be a source of anxiety for the British Government. The Secretary of State for India instructed Lord Dufferin several times to look after the Sindhanwalia Sardar. We are keeping the best watch over his actions that we can. But I do not like that man at Pondicherry and we shall have difficulty in preventing Dhuleep Singh joining him if so inclined."[8]

The Secretary of State for India was so much annoyed with Maharaja Dalip Singh that he did not even spare the family of the Maharaja. He called Prince Victor, the son of Maharaja, and asked him to discard the use of word "Maharajkumar" to which he readily agreed.

Since Russia was in alliance with France, England had its own apprehensions. Lord Cross wrote to Lord Dufferin:- "The renewal of military activities on the part of Russia in Central Asia is giving rise to apprehensions in England. Ruthless power that she is, she ought to be tried for disturbing the peace of the whole world."[9]

deGiers who was appointed to watch the activities of Maharaja Dalip Singh was in direct correspondence with the Secretary of State for India and his letters were passed on to Lord Dufferin. deGiers appears to have deputed somebody else to help him in this matter. His name was Roberts. Lord Cross wrote about these men in his confidential letter dated March 25, 1887. "The F.O. (deGiers) assures me that we may rely upon their information and also upon their informant. Meanwhile they wish us to do nothing either here or in England which arouses suspicion, but, of

107

course, Roberts will keep his eyes and ears open."[10]

From the personal letters of Lord Cross it appears certain that he did not like Thakur Singh Sindhanwalia as he himself refered to Lord Dufferin, "his friend in relations in Pondicherry". The other person who rankled in the eyes of the British Government was KatKoff, a Russian. He was editor of a newspaper in Moscow. Maharaja Dalip Singh was in correspondence with him and he was arranging Maharaja's visit to Russia. deGiers appears to have been instructed to deal with KatKoff and he was regularly reporting about him. Lord Cross wrote to Lord Dufferin in his letter dated April 5, 1887:- "we have heard nothing further as to Dhuleep Singh. F.O. deGiers seems to hold his own so far against the Moscow newspaper Editor who is Dhuleep's friend." Again he wrote on April 22, 1887:-

"The great struggle between deGiers and the Moscow newspaper Editor involves great issues. Salisbury tells me that at present it looks as if deGiers would hold his own. It would be a great blessings to Europe and to India if such should prove to be the case. Looking through the extracts of vernacular press which came before us, I do not gather from them that Dhuleep Singh can do much harm, but if deGiers aims, it is plain that he would not be allowed to go to Peterburg."[11]

The British Government wanted that the Maharaja should not be allowed to go to Russia. But the Maharaja had made up his mind. Mr KatKoff was arranging his visit to Russia with the help of Mr Patrick Casey.[12] It was under the latter's passport that Maharaja reached Berlin on route to St. Peterburg. He was accompanied by a Sikh named Aroor Singh. At the Central Station of Berlin on the 22nd March 1887 according to press correspondent of the *Daily Chronicles* "the satchal containing Maharaja's passport and 30,000 francs was abstracted by the British detectives" who were closely watching movements of the Maharaja. The latter did not lose heart, he telegraphed the account of his losing passport to KatKoff with whom he had been in correspondence. KatKoff asked the Maharaja to continue his journey and assured him that he would find a police permit waiting him on the border. Despite British

108

Government's best efforts to prevent the Maharaja to go to Moscow, he reached Moscow there early April 1887. Thus in the first round of struggle deGiers was defeated and KatKoff won. Lord Cross in his next letter to Lord Dufferin wrote on 28th, April, 1887: "Dhuleep Singh has, you see, gone to Russia. He has for some time under a feigned name at Moscow under KatKoff's auspices and there has evidently been a lot of contest between that gentleman and deGiers. I wrote to foreign office last night urging them to demonstrate on how Dhuleep Singh has thrown of his incognuits.....you will, of course, narrowly watch as to any effect produced in India by these proceedings".[13] Next day again he wrote to the Governor-General, "you would have heard of Dhuleep Singh's visit to Russia. He has been taken by KatKoff and is at Moscow."[14]

Petition to Russian Emperor

On May, 10, 1887, Maharaja Dalip Singh, addressed petition to the Emperor of Russia, wherein he wrote, "Through my cousin Sirdar Thakur Singh (a man well-known both in the Punjab and all over India) I have been deputed by most of the powerful Princes of India to come to Russia and pray that Imperial Government to take their cause in hand. These Princes possess altogether some 3,00,000 soldiers in their service and are prepared to revolt should the Imperial Government think proper to make and advance upon the British provided that I, their representative, be permitted to accompany the Imperial Army so as to assure them of the generous and gracious intentions entertained towards them by the Emperor."[15]

Lord Cross wrote to Lord Dufferin on June 2, 1887, "What will become of Dhuleep Singh, I do not know. He is evidently to be wild as mad tool by KatKoff. He is driving about Moscow every day in his best attire making a great show but hitherto Emperor has kept clear. How you have heard any thing of Thakur Singh and French subsidy. I shall wait your post with much interest."[16]

It is very significant to note that Lord Cross in his private letters lays stress on the struggle of deGiers, (F.O.) who was pursuing Maharaja Dalip Singh and KatKoff, the friend of the Maharaja. It is however, not clear, what the nature of this struggle

109

was, but Lord Cross refered to it in several of his letters. He wrote to Lord Dufferin on March 25, 1887, "The F.O. assures me that we may rely upon their information and also upon their informant."

"Meanwhile they wish us to do nothing either here or in England which could arouse suspicion but, of course, Roberts will keep his eyes and ears open." Again he wrote on 5th April 1887, "deGiers seems to hold his own so far against the Moscow newspaper Editor who is Dhuleep Singh's friend." He wrote on 22nd April 1887, "The great struggle between the Giers and the Moscow newspaper Editor envolves a great issue. Salisbury tells me that at present it looks as if deGiers would hold his own. It would be a great blessing to Europe and India if such should prove to be the case."[17] "There has evidently been lot of contest between that gentleman (KatKoff) and deGiers."[18] On 29th April he wrote, "you would have heard of Dhuleep's visit to Russia. He has been taken by KatKoff and is at Moscow. But we hope that deGiers will hold his own and if so all will be well." On 12th May, he asserted, "The struggle between deGiers and KatKoff still goes on."[19] This struggle however, ended in the death of KatKoff. Whether the British Government had any hand in it or how for deGiers was responsible for it cannot be established conclusively.

But Lord Cross frequent references to this struggle arouses suspicion as to the intentions of the British Government. Lord Cross was very happy to report the death of KatKoff to Lord Dufferin. He wrote, "KatKoff's death will materially interfere with his plans in Russia, and I cannot think that he will stay there long."[20] It is very significant to note that Thakur Singh Sindhanwalia about whom Lord Cross wrote to Dufferin that "I do not like that man at Pondicherry" also died at Pondicherry almost simultaneously. Again the circumstances about the death are not known, but these incidents were very favourable to the British Government. Lord Cross wrote in his letter of Sept. 16, 1887, "The star of Dhuleep Singh (if so ever there was) is not shining very bright at present. The deaths of KatKoff and his Pondicherry friend are weighty incidents."[21]

Another letter Lord Cross intimated to the Governor-General,

110

"I have received further private information about Dhuleep Singh who is evidently bitterly disappointed at the turn of things have taken in Russia and is talking to the effect that all is to be wretched peace."[22]

Maharaja's Source of Income?

Another aspect as to what was source of income of Maharaja Dalip Singh during his travels of Europe has not been discovered so far. Some of the letters of the Secretary of State suggest that Maharaja Dalip Singh might be receiving money from India. But he is not sure, he writes in his letter dated October 20, 1887, "I am given to understand that D. Singh has received money through Lala Jhilinda (?) Ram Phadev (?) at Multan and Sardar Delalnoun (?) Jang or Hyderabad."[23] Another letter he wrote, "Durand has sent an interesting letter to Bradford. He asks at the end of it whether Dhuleep Singh drew any money from England. My answer is certainly not. He does not draw any part of his allowance which is comfortably accummulating. He certainly gets nothing from the estates which are all managed by us. His wife's allowance is all in the hands of trustees and no money goes to him from this source."[24]

Lord Cross's private letters are important for writing last years of Maharaja Dalip Singh. They throw flood of light on various aspects of his life.

—Dr. Kirpal Singh

References

1. India Office Library, London, Eurp. Mss. 243 Vol. 17, page 108 microfilm no. 96 State Archives Patiala from the material brought from England by Dr Kirpal Singh.
2. India Office Library, London, Eurp. Mss. 243. Vol. 17, page 126.
3. Ibid. Vol. 17, page 160-161.
4. Ibid. page 27-28.
5. Ibid. page 153-54.
6. Lord Cross, letter of June 6, 1886, ibid, page 108.
7. Sardar Thakur Singh Sindhanwalia was the son of S. Lehna Singh Sindhanwalia. He was appointed an Extra Assistant Commissioner in 1865;

In 1877 he joined the Punjab Commission. He visited England in 1885 and remained nine month as the guest of Maharaja Dalip Singh. In 1886 shortly after his return to India he fled to Pondicherry where he died in 1887. Griffin writes that he died in Dec. 1887 *(Chiefs & Families of note in Punjab* Vol. II. page 411) but Lord Cross refers to his death in his letter Sept. 16, 1887.

8.   Ibid. Vol. 17, page 145.

9.   Ibid. Vol. 17, page 108.

10.   Ibid. Vol. 17, page 161.

11.   Ibid. page 178.

12.   *Maharaja Dalip Singh* by Dr Jagjit Singh, Type copy page 55.

13.   Microfilm No. 96, State Archives, Patiala, page 187.

14.   Ibid.

15.   *The Punjab Past and Present,* Punjabi University, Patiala Vol. II, page 252.

16.   Ibid. page 212.

17.   Ibid. pages, 161, 170, 178, 18.

18.   Ibid. page 183.

19.   Ibid. page 187.

20.   Ibid. page 264.

21.   Ibid. page 286.

22.   Letter dated 1st. Oct., 1887. Ibid. page 306.

23.   Ibid. page, 309.

24.   Ibid. page 187, letter dated 16th Sept. 1887.

Chapter IV

MAHARAJA DULEEP SINGH IN THE EYES OF THE NON-SIKHS :
A SURVEY OF INDIAN HISTORICAL TRADITION

In the Sikh studies we have been accustomed to listen to the following assertion of Lieutenant Colonel Malcolm : '[It] is of the most essential importance to hear what a nation has to say of itself.' We have thus been taught to regard the *Sakhi* literature as our indispensable guide to the reconstruction of the life and message of the founder of the Panth. Similarly, the *Gur Sobha* sources have equally been taken into consideration in outlining the development of the history and culture of the Sikhs of the subsequent centuries. But we occasionally come across dissenting voices regarding this version of Sikh sources. This has added newer dimensions in our understanding of the traditional Sikh ideals and institutions. It stimulates debate and a few leading organisations have come forward with a meaningful version of what they consider to be the 'authoritative and sober defence of Sikhism'.

Again the contribution of some British officials and scholars have no less been impressive in this field. Ganda Singh's *Early European Accounts of the Sikhs* (1962) is an index of their pioneering contributions. This branch of Sikh studies has continued to be enriched by the academicians of the West. Barrier's scholarly study introduces us to a significant area of this scholarly tradition while Dr. Trilochan Singh's posthumous work is sure to break a fresh ground of our understanding of the 'hypercritical' 'urbane' tradition of western scholarship.

While we have been keeping a close watch over the minutest details of what is being written in the West, are we equally conscious of what has been depicted in the different regional

113

languages of the Indian sub-continent of the last one hundred and fifty years? Perhaps, we are hardly aware of the vast source materials lying scattered in the different libraries and elsewhere. Many of us would agree that they perhaps constitute a neglected area of Sikh studies. We may be knowing a lot about the Sikhs of Southhall, Santa Barbra and Yuba Valley. Are we keeping ourselves in close touch with the Sikhs of Lanka, Barkola and Hathipara of the Brahmaputra Valley? Similarly, many of us are not aware of the contribution of an unknown *granthi* of the Bara Sangat Gurdwara of Calcutta who had helped Tinkari Banerjee in translating some sections of *Surajprakash* in Bengali. We have equally forgotten those people who restored the Kaliaboda Gurdwara (situated on the banks of the river Mahanadi in Cuttuck, built in memory of Guru Nanak's visit to Jagannath Puri) to its pristine purity on the *gurupurab* of 1935. Thus many of us may be reading the pioneering studies of Indubhushan Banerjee, Narendra Krishna Sinha and Anil Chandra Banerjee and regard them as isolated examples of Sikh historical tradition in eastern India. On the contrary, they had before them a long list of pioneers, many of whom still remain unknown to us. They come from different walks of life—poets, philosophers, political propagandists, travellers, journalists, religious reformers, novelists, dramatists and biographers. They outlined the lives of the Gurus, reconstructed the roles of the martyrs, analysed the achievements of the crownheads, reviewed the significance of the *Rahit Mariyada*, translated the sacred literatures, depicted the history of the leading gurudwaras and portrayed the struggling personalities of Sikh women in their mother tongue.

This non-Sikh perception of Sikh studies has its own importance when the Sikhs themselves have been coming into greater interactions with the non-Sikhs beyond Punjab. But these works are partially indebted to the colonial rule. As the British administration had steadily penetrated deep into the heart of the subcontinent, it introduced railways, made use of regional languages in local law courts and educational institutions, facilitated the development of native press stimulating dialogue among the vernacular elites of the presidency towns, *muffasil* headquarters and even beyond. Growing interactions at the different levels of the society in the perspective of India's struggle for freedom necessitated an urge for a new national identity based on shared or imagined experiences of the past. Vernacular press was destined to become an important vehicle of the pan Indian identity in which history was reconstructed and revised for the consumption of their own community.

Popularising the Message of Sikhism

This, however, does not tell the whole story. A century old Brahmo search for a separate and identical monotheistic tradition in Indian religious system, as we have seen elsewhere, also led to a quest for Sikh philosophy and religion. Actually, the Brahmos of Bengal and Orrisa played a pioneering role in popularising the message of Sikhism in this part of the country. Another fact was the repercussions of the different political developments of Punjab in the eastern India native press. Thus the experiences of the second Sikh war were frequently reported in the *Orunodoi* - the earliest Assamese monthly journal published from Sibsagar. They also kindled the poetic imagination of Ishwarchandra Gupta, editor of the *Sambad Prabhakar*. It would be no exaggeration to argue that the Akali struggle for the gurudwara reforms of the 1920s frequently hit the headlines of the various newspapers of Calcutta, Cuttuck, Dibrugarh, Guwahati, Patna and Puri. Prior to it, the activities of Maharaja Duleep Singh in India, England and the continent did not altogether miss the attention of the people. His death raised a storm of protest and his tragic end was frequently debated in the native press.

The non-Sikh perception of Maharaja Duleep Singh is nearly a century old process and it represents various shades of opinion. The dethroned king was both hailed and criticised by the authors who had tried to assess the royal role on the basis of their own understanding of the problem. We may get a glimpse of the author's individual bias which was often projected in his/her writings. Every historian is again a representative of his age and his analysis of the sources of history provides us a glimpse of the development of historiography in the region. Here we would be dealing with only two monographs : one written in Bengali while the other in Hindi.

They were both published from Calcutta which enjoys the proud privilege of bringing out *The Sikh Review* over nearly four decades. These works are separated from one another by nearly thirty years and review the Maharaja from two distinct standpoints at a time when the city itself had been experiencing a significant rise in the political barometer of the subcontinent.

Of the two works dealing with the life of Maharaja Duleep Singh, Barodakanta Mitra's monograph *Sikh Juddher Itihas O Maharaja Duleep Singha* was published first in 1893 and is still regarded to be an important landmark in the development of Bengali historiography on the Sikhs. The study may broadly be divided into two parts : the first one highlights the history of the Anglo-Sikh Wars, which, in the opinion of the author, marks 'the most decisive event' in the history of the nineteenth century India. The life of Maharaja Duleep Singh along with his fight for an honourable political settlement constitute the subject matter of the second part of the volume. It is still considered to be the most detailed account of Duleep Singh's life in Bengali. Divided into six chapters, this part reviews the career of Duleep Singh from 1849 (the year of his leaving Lahore for Fatehgarh) to 1893 (the year of his end in Paris). Regarding his sources, Mitra made no secret of his preference for Lady Login's writings. A careful reader cannot fail to notice the reference to the Maharaja's early enthusiasm for Christianity, his willingness to go to England, and after his mother's death, his growing disillusionment with the British are primarily based on Lady Login's observations. The author also drew frequently from the contemporary newspapers like the *Times, Moscow News, Statesman* and *Englishman* while reconstructing the pages of the Maharaja's closing days. The *Tribune* is however missing in the Bibliography. But what distinguishes Mitra's study is his awareness of the importance of the official sources like the parliamentary papers and the official dispatches which do not find their rightful place in any other writing on Sikh history in Bengali.

Mitra's volume also merits attention owing to its analytical projection of the changes in the relationship between the Maharaja and the Queen Mother Jindan over the years. Here again he seems to have broadly followed Lady Login's account and acknowledges his debt in the footnotes. The biographer finds that the young Duleep was not very sorry when he was first separated from his mother. Later on when he was in England, as the news of the mother's plight started reaching his desk, he became increasingly restless and developed a longing for her. When Duleep gradually grew up to be a matured man, Mitra argues, he tried to remain close to his mother, and the relationship became warm. The Queen made her son conscious of his royal heritage as well as of his association with the Panth. Mitra could bring out the Mother's profound influence upon her son whose readiness to set sail to India for cremating the mother's earthly remains add a human touch to this volume.

The historian has reviewed the relation between the Maharaja and the English administration with an equal skill. He points out the cause of complaint with a mixed touch of sympathy and melancholy. But the author does not seem to be happy with the Maharaja's decision of coming out of British political influence, nor does he ever find any justification in the latter's momentous declaration of taking the *Pahul* again in Punjab and the charges against the India council's vacillating policy on the settlement of his different financial claims. Mitra writes favourably about the Maharaja so long as he did not challenge the British authority in India and sympathises with him so long as the debate with the home Government was going on behind the scene. Later on when the Maharaja was criticising the English in public, he is no longer friendly towards him. His early sympathy evaporates and a sullen frame of mind takes its place. His loyalty towards the Crown perhaps affects his historical judgement and partially explains some of his uncharitable comments on Duleep Singh's fight for freedom in the Continent. Since the security and continuation of British rule in India constituted the cornerstone of his scheme of history, the policies which, in his opinion, would affect the British position in the sub-continent, would hardly evoke any favourable reception. This also largely explains his earlier accusations of Lord Dalhousie for his aggressive policy leading to the Sepoy Mutiny in the middle of the nineteenth century.

117

Critical Assessment about Duleep Singh

Mitra's sympathy for British rule as well as his criticism of the Maharaja were largely an outcome of the conditions under which he had undertaken the task of writing history in the last decade of the nineteenth century. The author belonged to a traditional and respectable family of north Calcutta known for their loyalty and support to British rule in the region. He inherited his family conviction and believed in the regenerating effect of the presence of the British in the country. Incidentally, these were the days when the Congress moderates were talking about imperial blessings and goodwill from the Congress platform. They could hardly dream of an end to British authority in India and generally asked for certain changes in Indian administration through constitutional means. Mitra's scheme of history thus fits in well with the intellectual climate of the presidency towns centering around the prevailing Congress politics of the period and he was well-disposed towards the Sikh monarch so long as he was not in conflict with this basic calculation about British rule in India. But the Maharaja's bitterness towards the English resulted in a corresponding change in his attitude.

Mitra's study, however, merits attention on two points: it surpassed all other previous works on Sikh history in its analytical treatment of the various categories of sources and it provided Bengali readership for the first time a biography of the Sikh monarch who was going to be hailed as a martyr in the succeeding decades of the next century. Inspite of its cool reception in the contemporary press, the book was destined to serve as a model before those who were going to undertake any study on the life and achievements of Maharaja Duleep Singh in the next century.

In the present century, as the nationalist movement took a tumultuous turn, vernacular elites could hardly remain satisfied with Mitra's assessment about Maharaja Duleep Singh. There was a growing need for redrawing the portrait with a nationalist colour, re-evaluating his relationship with the British government and re-examining his role in the Continent. In the native press, a new genre of literature was increasingly brought out highlighting the

118

contemporary nationalistic and patriotic sentiment. Consequently, the history of the Maharaja was given a glow of martyrdom—a dimension missing in the study of Mitra. They also provided a greater emphasis on issues like the ill-treatment meted out to the Sikh ruler by the Home Government, his tragic end in Paris in the midst of poverty and suffering. Duleep Singh's humiliation at the hands of the Home Government was compared with that of the Indians under British rule. This sentiment did not figure in the writings of Mitra. Instead of maintaining a silence like Mitra, they made no secret of their sympathy and support for the Sikh monarch and often narrated the course of events as his defence counsellor in the court of law.

In this category of writings, Nandkumardev Sharma's *Punjab Haran aur Maharaja Duleep Singh (1921)* merits special attention. It was written in Hindi; the author was long associated with the Hindi nationalist press of northern and eastern India and wrote a few popular biographies of the nationlist leaders. He had a genuine regard for the study of Indian history, though he had no formal training at the college/university level. History, according to him, had a regenerating power of its own and its meaningful study would help us understand the distinctiveness of Indian character, heritage and identity. 'It should be read', he pointed out, 'for learning lessons from our past failures' and 'stimulating a sense of national solidarity' in 'our struggle against British rule in India'. With these ends in view, Nandkumardev initiated his review of the history of the Sikhs. He had been contemplating of writing a history of the Sikhs since 1906 when he was in Lahore as a journalist with a local newspaper. He gradually acquainted himself with the different well-known secondary sources of Sikh history and published two monographs in 1914 and 1920 outlining the evolution of the Panth since the birth of Guru Nanak till the annexation of Punjab. His studies carried a deep note of patriotic sentiment and highlighted the martial tradition of the Sikhs in their resistance against the Mughals and the British. He was of the opinion that the Khalsa was defeated owing to the selfishness of the Sardars as well as of lack of unity among a larger number of Sikhs. He, therefore, urged upon the Sikhs of his generation for presenting a combined resistance against the British in India.

His third study is the *Punjab Haran* which brings out the profile of young Duleep Singh in the background of the annexation of Punjab after the Second Sikh War. Unlike Mitra, Sharma begins his account of Duleep Singh with all sympathy and argues that he fell a prey to British evil designs in the sub-continent. He was extremely critical about the British presence in India and underlined the need for Sikh support in resisting the colonial masters in that region. There is very little doubt that the prevailing political situation of the country must have played a decisive part in formulating his own plan of history and a brief reference to it would not be altogether irrelevant here.

Incidently, these were the years when resistance against British authority had already attained a crucial stage under the leadership of Gandhi ji. Punjab had witnessed the ravages of the Rowlatt Satyagraha and the Jallianawala massacre. The Sikhs were all bitter after the World War I owing to different reasons and, therefore, were setting the ground ready for the Akali-led Gurdwara Reform Movement leading to the birth of the SGPC in the 1920s. Above all, there was the Non-Cooperation Movement which was destined to engulf the whole of India and carried the national struggle to a higher level never reached before. It is nothing unusual that Sharma's volume would be reflecting a bitter anti-British nationalist sentiment through Duleep Singh's struggle against the Home Government and the Britishers in India. Thus, a sea change had taken place in the political horizon since Mitra had completed his study nearly three decades ago.

Fighter for Freedom

Sharma's Duleep Singh was fighter for freedom from the British hegemony; his crusade in the Continent represents an early phase of India's struggle for independence in the nineteenth century. Thus, an identity of emotion and aspiration between the historian and his study of history brought to life "the dead hands of the past". The Sikh monarch's fight with the English no longer remained a story of the distant past, but Sharma the historian was going to present it almost in the context of the early 1920s when

120

the Akalis themselves would be fighting for their gurdwaras and the deposed monarch of Nabha. Here history joins hands with the contemporary Indian political climate in which Duleep Singh's resistance and martyrdom came to be remembered again and again while championing the cause of another deposed monarch, namely, Ripudaman Singh. In this scheme of historiography, James Davy Cunningham and Evans Bell were to enjoy a place of honour and respect. Cunningham in particular was almost universally admired in the native press. While Mitra might have some complaints against Cunningham, Sharma in his preface made him the symbol of historical honesty owing to his sufferings and insult at the hands of the colonial administration. Hence Sharma's Cunningham was very dear to the Indian nationalist historiographical tradition and, therefore, translations of Cunningham's study in different regional languages were nothing unusual.

—**Himadri Banerjee**

Chapter V

THE REBELLIOUS MAHARAJA

Maharaja Duleep Singh is the least published and publicised name of the Maharajas in the times of British India. This has been so because the British, who usurped his kingdom ensured that his name was kept in oblivion and out of the records and whatever was kept on record was to negate his claims. They succeeded in containing the Sikh rebellion against them and an easy run through over the Sikh psyche.

However, with the departure of the British from the scene and with the increasing efforts to find out the lost pages of the Sikh history the emerging facts are giving new shapes to the history. Maharaja Duleep Singh, son of the Great Maharaja of Punjab, Maharaja Ranjit Singh turns out to be a fiery young man who put up tremendous fight against all odds to gain his lost kingdom and freedom for his people from the usurpers of his rule. Even though much water had flowed between the time he lost his kingdom as a child and the time he grew up to understand the effects of the great loss, yet he tried to make up the same with his diligent and relentless effort. If he failed, it is not because of his effort but because of the watchful hawk-eyes and effective propaganda machinery of the British who ensured his isolation from Punjab and seclusion from his relatives and well-wishers. Further the misinformation compaign they launched against him depicting him a pleasure-seeking, contended Christian, succeeded immensely in the light of no other information reaching the Punjab people.

He was enthroned at the age of five on September 18, 1843 after the tragic death of his brother Maharaja Sher Singh[1]. He had to singly face the onslaught of the disloyal courtiers and the overpowering British from the very young age as he was even

122

deprived of the protection of his mother. Though Maharani Jind Kaur was appointed his Regent yet the actual authority had passed from the palace to the cantonment and the military panchayats[2] as the Queen Mother was virtually abducted and kept in prison or exile throughout her later life.

The British provoked the Sikhs in December 1845, by annexing the territories of Lahore Darbar on the left bank of the Sutluj, culminating into the first Anglo-Sikh War and into concluding a peace treaty on March 9, 1846 whereby the victorious British occupied the fertile Jalandhar Doab, the hills of Jammu and the Valley of Kashmir. More stringent terms were imposed on December 16, 1846 in the Treaty of Bhyrowal, reducing the kingdom of Punjab to a virtual protectorate. The Regent was pensioned off, the Regency passing on to the British. To remove impediments in their free rule, the British imprisoned the Queen Mother Maharani Jind Kaur into Suman Burj and separated Duleep Singh from her[3]. A sense of fear was gradually instilled into his mind to cause permanent subjugation and destroy any influence of his mother. *Aj Maharaj (Duleep Singh) sade pass ake bahut ronde rahe ne. Aakhan lagge, sahnu Bishan Singh te Gulabh Singh draunde ne.* (Today Maharaj (Duleep Singh) wailed and cried. He complained Bishan Singh and Gulabh Singh were threatening him). These extracts from the letter from Maharani Jind Kaur to the British Resident at Lahore, Henry Lawrence in August 1847[4] and other letters make clear mention that the child Maharaja Duleep Singh was put under constant pressure to accept total subjugation to the British and to forget his origin.

After the Second Anglo-Sikh war (1848-49), the ten-year-old Maharaja Duleep Singh was deprived of his crown and the kingdom and the Punjab was annexed to the British dominions. The custody of the Maharaja was passed onto Dr. John Login under whom he was shifted to Fatehgarh (U.P.) by Feb 16, 1850. Only Christians and Christianity oriented Hindus and no Sikhs were allowed to meet him since his departure from Lahore or thereafter[5]. Not only Maharani Jind Kaur but the other freedom loving Sikhs saw to the game of the British. The Maharani sought the assistance of the great freedom fighter Maharaj Singh in January 1850[6] through her confidant Prema to liberate the young Maharaja from the British. The plan leaked out,

Prema arrested and summons issued against Maharaj Singh[7]. Ultimately on March 8, 1853 at the age of 15, the British snatched away from the Maharaja his identity as a Sikh. He was converted to Christianity and transported to Britain, severing all his links from his mother, motherland, kingdom and religion[8].

Lured into Extravagant Life-style

He was lured into an extravagant style of Victorian English nobility[9] to make him forget all his past. The British propagated every event of his frugality to declare that 'Maharaja Duleep Singh was a frugal and lavish prince who was a guiding light for the other princes to live as a true Christian and the loyal subject of Her Majesty, the Queen of England.'

But the Maharaja rarely forgot his past. His rebellious spirit never gave up and he displayed kingly behaviour throughout his life. On 7th August 1847 when he was asked by the British to apply 'tilak' on the forehead of the renegade Tej Singh the child Maharaja refused the action which later resulted in banishment of Maharani Jind Kaur[10]. Lady Login recorded that he would sometimes refuse to act as desired by his tutor Dr. John Login. According to her, when he ran out into the garden during a heavy downpour, he got thoroughly drenched. "Finding him in this condition Login wished him to change his clothes, but half in play, the boy said he would do so at the usual time, and when urged to change at once, he turned obstinate."[11] In another incidence, when he was being taken to Fatehgarh, he insisted on taking a dip in the Ganges near Hardwar. The British officers accompanying him as escort refused permission. They had however to relent and he was allowed to take bath at Kankhal a few miles downstream.[12]

The British in India were always conscious of the fact of Maharaja's impending influence on Indians. Lord Dalhousie claimed that 'with (his) conversion, political influence of the Maharaja had been destroyed forever' (Lord Dalhousie to Dr. Login, 23rd July 1851). However he always thought of any remote influence of Sikhism on the Maharaja and wrote to Sir George Cooper on October 11, 1854, 'The nightcappy appearance of his turban is his strongest national feature. Do away with that and he has no longer any outward and visible sign of a Sikh about him.' But the Maharaja started asserting himself as he grew up. When he refused to marry the Princess Gouramma of Coorg stating that, 'I could never marry her'[13] it was an indication of the things to come.

He studied the Parliamentary papers (Blue Books) in the British museum and came across primary and secondary evidence and was soon convinced that the British had illegally deprived him of his kingdom of Punjab.[14]

Things changed in 1859, when his mother Maharani Jind Kaur was allowed to meet the Maharaja at Rani Gunj, Calcutta and later allowed to shift to England to stay with her son. The bitter mother had been kept in prison in Suman Burj, Sheikhupura (May 17, 1848 onwards), Benaras (April 3, 1849 onwards) and Chunar from where she escaped on 21 April 1849 to Nepal and reached Kathmandu on April 29[15]. She established secret correspondence with her son through her agents at Amritsar and Patna. As the correspondence between the two was disclosed, the British did not find much in the letters confiscated and on a request from the Maharaja allowed him to meet the ageing Maharani at Calcutta. Later the Maharani was allowed to stay in England where she shifted first in Mulgrave Castle and then in London where they stayed together from 1861 to 1863.[16] 'The only thing which she could do during this period was to remind her son of his duty to his country and his religion' which she did perfectly.

Mother's Influence

She reminded him of his past, his position, his ancestors and the treacheries of the British and the courtiers. She praised the Sikh religion and the Maharaja showed signs of drifting away from his new faith, forced upon him in childhood. The impressions of the Maharani on Duleep Singh were rightly stated in *The Times* of August 31, 1882. "The Maharaja was able to put in perspective the perfidious, illegal and immoral acts of the British rulers during his infancy and minority, and let the public know how the terms of the Bhyrowal Treaty were grossly abused and the Maharaja unjustly deprived of his kingdom"[17]. Lady Login wrote; "the Maharaja's religious feelings were at this time in an unsettled and emotional condition, attracted by the most extravagant and ignorant forms of sectarianism, so that one never knew from day to day what fresh idea he might be pursuing," and that the Maharaja was "getting thoroughly under his mother's influence".[18]

On August 1, 1861, the Maharaja wrote to John Login from Auchlyne, to immediately request permission from the Indian authorities for his return to that country along with his mother, giving up all his claims except the one in Dehradun where he wanted to settle. The broken-hearted Maharani who had an earnest desire to return to her motherland with her son waited for the decision of the Indian authorities but no confirmation came. With ill-health, dim eyesight and torn dreams she left for her heavenly abode on August 1, 1863. The dead body was temporarily placed in a vault in Kensal Green Cemetery until the permission was granted for her transportation to India for her burial at Benaras as per her last wish. The body of Maharani Jind Kaur landed at Bombay under the superintendence of Kishen Singh and Achhar Singh. At the Bombay port, soldiers of Balauch Regiment were posted for protection. 'They however, on seeing the Maharaja and the body of the late Maharani, got violent and raised provocative slogans eulogising the Maharaja. Sensing trouble, the superintendent and the commissioner stopped the body from proceeding to Benaras and the burial was ordered to be completed at Nasik. Maharaja Duleep Singh was infuriated and had a hand-to-hand scuffle with the senior most official present. The British who did not want to take any chance, prevented him to go to Hardwar and ultimately the last rites were performed at Nasik on the bank of Godavri, where a monument and a Gurdwara were erected in her memory. A village was purchased and allotted for the expenses of these two. This monument could be seen on the bank of Godavri close to the place where now an idol of Sri Hanuman is erected. The monument was razed to the ground by the municipality around 1952 A.D. The Gurdwara still exists.'[19] Maharani Jind Kaur, in her brief contact instilled in him the tenets of Sikhism and an eagerness to retake his lost kingdom.

The fire was further incensed in the year 1884 when he came in contact with his collateral Sardar Thakur Singh Sandhanwalia in connection with his claims for the properties in India. Sardar Thakur

126

Singh who stayed with him for about 9 months in 1884-85, gradually reminded him of his past and initiated him into the tenets of Sikhism. He daily read out from the holy *Guru Granth Sahib* to the Prince and repeatedly reminded the Maharaja that, 'He was a King and he would be a King' and 'the whole of Punjab wanted him'.[20]

Thakur Singh had also brought with him a document signed by the Jathedars of Takhats (the highest ecclesiastical seats) which contained the following prophecy: "He (Duleep Singh) will drive his elephant throughout the world... Dissension will arise at Calcutta and quarrels will be in every home. Nothing will be known for 12 years. Then will rise the Khalsa whom the people of four castes will like... Fighting will take place near Delhi... When Delhi will remain 15 kos away, the King will cease. Duleep Singh will sit on the throne and all people will pay him homage." Thakur Singh also had got the permission from the five high priests for his re-conversion to Sikhism[21].

His mother's sustained though short indoctrination, Thakur Singh's orientation and the letter from the high Priests changed his thinking process firing his imagination. He became eager to return to Punjab and to assert himself. He could no more bear the burden of Christianity and wanted to rebaptise into Sikhism, the religion of his ancestors. One day as soon as the Maharaja got out of his bed, he asked Thakur Singh to baptise him as a Sikh, saying that the soul of Guru Gobind Singh had visited him on the previous night and had commanded him to be ready. He was further encouraged by the letters received from his kins and other Indians showing their allegiance and concern towards him. When Sardar Sant Singh, brother-in-law of Rani Jind Kaur offered his services, the Maharaja wrote back on 7th Oct. 1885, "...As the British Govornment refuse to do me justice, therefore, I shall leave England on the 16th of December next and take up my residence quietly at Delhi ...As you are aware by this time that I have rejoined the faith of my ancestors, I salute you with *Wah Gooroo ji dee Fateh...*"[22]

The Maharaja was not allowed to leave in December 1885 as planned. Another reply by the Maharaja dated March 9th 1886 to the enquiries from Punjab gives the indications of the British highhandedness, "I am very pleased to receive your letter, but I advise you not to come near me without permission of Government as you might get into trouble with the authorities. I intend to leave England with my family on 31st of this month but it is possible a little delay may occur. I need not tell you how pleased I shall be for you to be present at my receiving 'Powl' which I trust my cousin Thakur Singh Sandhanwalia will administer to me. I am now longing to return to India although Government are afraid to let me reside in the North-Western Provinces and desire me to live at Ootacamund but I put my faith entirely to Satgooroo, who now that I turn to him for forgiveness, I know not forsake me."[23]

Letter to Countrymen

On 25th March 1886, the Maharaja released the following letter to his countrymen. "My beloved countrymen ....I submit to His Will; being persuaded that whatever is for the best will happen. I now, therefore, beg forgiveness of you, Khalsa jee or the Pure; for having forsaken the faith of my ancestors for a foreign religion... It is my fond desire on reaching Bombay to take *pahul* again, and I sincerely hope for your prayer to the Sutgooroo on the solemn occasion. But in returning to the faith of my ancestors, you must clearly understand, Khalsa jee, I have no intention of conforming to the errors introduced into Sikhism by those who were not true Sikhs— such for instance, as wretched caste observances, but to worship the pure and beautiful tenets of Baba Nanak and obey the commands of Gooroo Gobind Singh. I am compelled to write this to you because I am not permitted to visit you in Punjab, as I had much hoped to do... I remain, my beloved countrymen, your flesh and blood."[24] Before starting, he invited Thakur Singh to meet him at Bombay and arrange for his re-initiation into Sikhism[25].

The news of arrival of the Maharaja into India caused great enthusiasm in the Indian public but the Indian Government considered his letters to his relatives and to the Indian papers as provocative. Handbills and books had been printed in which the coming back of the Maharaja was given wide publicity. The dream of restoring Khalsa Raj survived. The result was that, 'a village in the Lahore district refused to pay its land revenues saying that the tribute was due only to the King (Duleep Singh) who was shortly to arrive in India'[26].

Though the general public eagerly awaited the arrival, yet the key functionaries in the Government and the Sardars who had benefited from the treacheries against the Sikh Raj became apprehensive at the news. Col Hennessy CO 15 Sikh informed the Government in Feb. 1886, "The spirit of the Sikhs is not dead and they are full of national fire. I should tremble in my shoes were that gentleman (Mahraja Duleep Singh) to arrive at our borders with Russians. The British Government should hold him fast secure in England in my opinion."[27] A letter published on March 25, 1886 alarmed the Military Department who wrote to the Adjutant General to ascertain the feelings of the Punjab troops. The C-in-C wrote to the Viceroy, "...I always thought that the return or even the threatened return of Duleep Singh to India would raise hopes of a revival of power amongst certain sections of the Sikhs and his presence with a Russian force in Afghanistan might cause some trouble with the Sikh soldiers." He again wrote to Lord North-Brook that "Duleep Singh's proposed visit to India has caused some excitement among the restless spirit of the Punjab.."[28] Even the Queen of England was apprehensive. On August 15, 1885, Posonby wrote to Lord Churchill that "the Maharaja may take some steps which may lead to serious consequences."[29].

Apprehensions of British Government

The apprehensions of the Indian Government if seen in the overall situation then prevailing in the world in general and India in particular would reveal the following:-

1. France and Germany were creating trouble in Egypt and Turkey against the British, through Islamite League and Wahabis.

2. The Irish nationalists were sympathetically disposed towards the Maharaja and an Irish Finian, a retired Major from the British Army, joined with the Maharaja in his purpose.

3. In India upper class Mohammedans with the backing of influential persons like the Beghum of Bhopal and her husband Nawab Sadiq Hussain were also active against the British.

4. The activities of Maharaj Singh and Ram Singh Bhaini and the

Kuka movement under him were truly disposed towards the Maharaja and against the British. A great disaffection against the British Raj was being created in Punjab and a strong uprising was expected.

Meanwhile the Maharaja started writing letters to India about his feelings. He wrote to the princes and nobles in 1886, "Brother Princes and Nobles and the people of beloved Hindustan. By the Grace of Almighty God, the Creator of the universe, the most merciful and gracious, and of Sri Guru Gobind Singh Ji, We, Maharaj Duleep Singh, the lawful sovereign of the Sikh Nation, have set aside and annulled that treaty of annexation of the Punjab, to the disgrace of Great Britain, be it said, was extorted from us and our Darbar, when we were of tender age, and ward of Christian England under the treaty of Bhyrowal 1846 (in order to lay his wicked hands on our dominions) by the late unscrupulous Marquis of Dalhousie. But the British nation is no respector of 'Solemn covenants' and treaties when its own interests are at variance with the interests of the weaker contracting parties there to; as most of you as well as ourselves know by experience. No doubt your mighty rulers will call upon you to refute the above assertion, but dare they deny that it is not in their hearts what that leading journal in England 'The Times' not very long ago advocated, viz., the abolition of your armies, the maintenance of which is dearer to you than the life itself. The Government of India out of spite may indeed put its veto upon the generous impulse of your hearts, but if you all unite, it will be powerless to harm you... Hence be not cowards but brave and worthy of your great forefathers."[30]

He wrote another proclamation to his countrymen on February 7, 1886: "Courage! Courage! Courage! We your flesh and blood tell you, lift up your bowed down heads and drooping hearts for your redemption draweth near and by help of the almighty, Aryavarta shall once more be free and the rising. 'Young India' shall enjoy both liberty and self government... Sri Khalsa Ji, we exhort you to study the *Sakhees* and learn therein your glorious destiny as predicted by Dasam Padshah Sri Guru Gobind Singh Ji."[31]

Considering the situation before he left for India, he was warned that he must live where the Government of India decide (most likely Kodaikanal or Ootacammand) on pain of action under Regulations III of 1818[32]. The Maharaja was ready for the arrest as is apparent from his letter dated 2nd Nov. 1885 to Lord Churchill, "I welcome the official prosecution which awaits me in India..."[33] As he was determined to reach Delhi Sir Owen Burne's meeting with the Maharaja Duleep Singh mentions of the strong will of the Maharaja and his own knowledge of the effects of his reaching India, "If they touch me, it will shake the Punjab, if not now, at any rate later on. I am determined to go."[34] Despite of all the opposition, the Maharaja managed to start for India on March 31, 1886 along with his family on S.S. Verona to settle down at Delhi.

The Secretary of State sent a telegram to the Viceroy on 31st March 1886 (India Office Records collected by K.S. Thapar), "..In recent communication with Political Secretary (Sir Owen Burne) he (Maharaja) has used language of menacing character, referring to eventual troubles in India, war with Russia and the part he may take as head of the Sikh Nation. An address from him to Sikhs is stated to have been sent to India, just published in newspapers and since acknowledged by Maharaja to be genuine. It announces his intention to be re-baptised into Sikh faith, with a view to take his blessings as Gooroo of nation. Maharaja lays stress on text of alleged prophecy, announces successive steps by which he is to be restored to power. He no doubt intends to circulate this in India. Affair if neglected might possibly give serious trouble but I have no doubt you will take whatever measure you may deem necessary to prevent any dangerous feelings being excited among Sikhs. Dalip Singh's communications should be carefully watched. He is in a new state of mind which seems to border on mono-mania."

Arrested at Aden

On reaching Aden on 21st April 1886 the Maharaja was arrested from the ship by Brigadier General A.S.T. Hogg, British Resident at Aden, under regulation III of 1818. The news of his arrest was kept secret by the British but this information was given by the Maharaja to *The Times of India* as follows, "I was arrested at Aden without a warrant for arrest, and such a warrant was issued when I while staying at Aden, had re-embraced Sikh religion...Although the

Indian Government succeeded in preventing me from reaching Bombay lately, yet they are not able to close all the roads that there are to India, for when I return I can either land at Goa & Pondicherry, or if I fancy an overland route where I can enter the Punjab through Russia."[35]. When questioned in Parliament (Hansard: Parliamentary Proceedings) about the arrest, Mr. E.S. Howard, Under Secretary for India, stated, "....it is a fact that Maharaja Dalip Singh has been arrested at Aden. Arrangements had been made for his residence at a place in Southern India designated by the Viceroy, but the issue by the Maharaja of an inflammatory address to the Sikh Nation added to certain other declarations by him of a somewhat menacing character rendered it necessary, in the opinion of the Government of India to put in force the special powers possessed by the Governor-General-in-Council as soon as the Maharaja came within their jurisdiction at Aden."

Maharaja stayed at Aden for 43 days where he was lodged in the house of the Resident. Though the Maharaja referred to himself as prisoner but the British objected to the use of this word stating that he was free to go back to Europe. He asked for his servants waiting at Bombay (Jawand Singh of Burki and Thakur Singh of Wagah) who were despatched after a protracted correspondence with the Viceroy. As the Maharaja insisted on getting re-baptised into Sikhism, the two above, his servant Aroor Singh and two Sikhs from a Sikh Regiment which was returning from a battlefield in Europe[36] baptised him into Sikhism on May 25, 1886[37]. After further correspondence with the Viceroy, the Viceroy ordered that Dalip Singh may be allowed to go to Europe unconditionally (Viceroy to Resident Aden, Telegrams dated 30 May and 1 June 1886). Maharaja Dalip Singh asked the Viceroy and the Queen for his public trial but he received no communication. The Maharaja was outraged in his tenderest point and furious at the insult offered to him and he drafted his rebellious manifesto signing himself on board the ship returning from Aden as "Lawful Soveregin of the Sikh Nation", etc.

Feeling insulted, Duleep Singh resigned his allowance and forswore fealty to the British crown. He gave up his English citizenship. He telegraphed to the Viceroy, "I return to Europe from 1st July next. I resign stipend paid to me under Treaty of Annexation, thus laying aside that iniquitous document."[38] He did not settle back in England; instead he reached Paris on 3 June 1886[39] from where he wrote a detailed letter of his decisions to Government of India on 15th July 1886: "By the Grace of Sri Sat Guru Ji; we the Maharaja Duleep Singh, the lawful Sovereign of the Sikh Nation, under the Treaty of Bhyrowal entered into 'without coercion' between ourselves and our Darbar on the one part and Great Britain on the other, do from hereby in consequence of the insults and indignities repeatedly offered to us, of whom the recent imprisonment inflicted on us at Aden is a proof as well as on the account of non fulfilment with us on stipulation, set aside and annul that iniquitous and illegal document the so-called 'Terms Granted', which was extorted from us in 1849 by our wicked Guardian, the Christian British nation, when we were an infant of only 11 years of age, and by the above first mentioned comment, under the protection of England"[40].

At Paris, he became very active to regain his lost kingdom and became totally rebellious to what all was ingrained into his mind by the British over a long period. Towards this end, he wrote letters to various princes and nobles in India inciting them to rise united against the British, sent his emissaries to establish contacts with those who could help establish a government in exile in French territories.

Since Russia was in alliance with France, and had interests in Afghanistan and Punjab, the Maharaja considered Russia as a would-be ally against the British. The events of the period and Sandhanwalia's appreciation led him to strongly believe that Russians were against the British and the time was not very far when a war would start between England and Russia on the question of liberation of India. Russia stood against the British in Crimean War (1854-56) and Afghan Wars (1839-42 & 1878-1881). The British too believed that the steady advance of Russia towards Herat in Afghanistan would one day lead to Russian invasion of India. Prof. William Langer writes, "There was a talk of Russian advance as far as the important fortified town of Herat and of far reaching schemes directed against India."[41] Prof. Michael T. Florinsky wrote, "On March 30, 1885 there occurred a bloody battle near Ak-Teppe in which the Afghans were defeated. Although Ak-Teppe affair took place in violation of instructions received from St. Petersburg, it is interpreted in London as evidence of Russia's bad faith.The countries appear to be on the verge of war. Giers requested Germany to fulfil her treaty obligations. Gladstone obtained from parliament large credits for Defence of India."[42]

Under these conditions, Maharaja rightly expected that his alliance with the Russians would be to his advantage. With the assistance of Sheik Jamal-ud-din and Abdul Rashid he contacted Russian Ambassador at Paris, Kotezbue, immediately after his return from Aden. The Russian Ambassador Kotezbue and Foreign Minister DeGiers did not co-operate, instead they discouraged him since they did not want to spoil relations with the mighty British. This is apparent from Kotezbue's letter to DeGiers dated 5/17 July 1886 and 30 July/10 August 1886 and to the Maharaja on 16/28 July 1886[43]. Though the Russian Foreign Office, as also DeGiers, not only discouraged but also resisted and created impediments in Maharaja's contacts and departure for Russia, it was Mikhail Nikioforovich Katkoff, editor of Moscow Gazette and a very strong supporter of Russian Expansionist Party who helped the Maharaja visit Russia with the help of Mr. Patrick Casey, an Irish revolutionary, on whose passport the Maharaja visited Russia[44]. The British too did not want the Maharaja to have contacts with Russians or to go to Russia. They detailed dedicated detectives like Roberts who kept regular watch on him under Lord Cross's directions and had put pressure on DeGiers in stopping him coming to Russia.

Establishes Government in Exile

Not seeing much progress with the Russians initially the Maharaja opened another front. On Jan 10, 1887, the Maharaja announced the establishment of emigre Government at Pondicherry with Thakur Singh as his Prime Minister.[45] Pondicherry being under the French was safer. Thakur Singh Sandhanwalia slipped into Pondicherry soon after and established 'Punjab Government-in-Exile'. The British Government was alarmed. The Secretary of State for India, Lord Cross instructed Lord Dufferin, the Viceroy of India to have strict watch on the Sandhanwalia Sardar. In his letter dated March 9, 1887 he wrote, "I am not quite easy about Duleep Singh. We are keeping as best watch over his actions that we can, but I do not like that man at Pondicherry and we shall have difficulty in preventing Duleep Singh joining him if he is so inclined."[46]

From Pondicherry, Sandhanwalia masterminded the operations on behalf of Maharaja Duleep Singh. To win support for the cause he visited secretly the Indian princely states and the Sikh shrines. He maintained active liaison with people in distant places through a chain of servants, dependants and relations. Major Bell's book *'The Annexation of the Punjab and the Maharaja Duleep Singh'* exhibiting the illegality and immorality of British occupation of the Punjab, was widely circulated.[47] Before departing for Russia the Maharaja sent instructions to Thakur Singh through his most faithful servant Aroor Singh. These include instructions by Maharaja to 'wage a war on the British to liberate his country'. Thakur Singh Sandhanwalia's sons Gurdit Singh and Narinder Singh helped and later his third son Gurbachan Singh, an Assistant Commissioner in Punjab, also resigned and joined him to pursue the cause. They all settled in Pondicherry where from they carried out all activities[48].

The letters from the Maharaja brought by Aroor Singh included letters to the ex-kings of Oudh, Holkar, Scindia, and the rulers of Patiala, Nabha, Faridkot, Jind and Kapurthala. The princes generally implicated in the cause were Raja Bikaram Singh of Faridkot, Raja Hira Singh of Nabha, the Maharaja of Kashmir, and Raja Moti Singh of Punchh. From Russia Duleep Singh sent to Thakur Singh a seal and a letter in token of his appointment to the office of prime minister, "I appoint you my Prime Minister should Sri Satguru Ji one day replace me on the throne of Punjab"[49].

With the help of his friends Katkoff and Patrick Casey the Maharaja left Paris on 21st March 1887 for St. Petersburg to seek the help of Tzar in liberation of India and specifically the Punjab. The British Secret Service kept a regular watch on him during his move and tried to stall his reaching Russia by all possible means. According to the press correspondent of *Daily Chronicle,* on 22 March 1887 at Berlin when the Maharaja was proceeding to Russia 'the satchel containing Maharaja's passport and 30,000 francs was abstracted by the British detectives'. Katkoff again helped him with a police passport at the border with the help of General Bogdanovitch. Despite the efforts of the British to stop him, the

Maharaja reached Moscow in April 1887 and remained under a feigned name for sometime.

Maharaja stayed for nearly 20 months in Russia. After reaching Russia he met Katkoff and held secret meetings for planning for the future. He established communication with Russian Emperor Alexander III and sought an interview which did not materialise due to the interference by Giers. Maharaja's long letter to the Tzar which was duly commented by the Russian King is the only notable event of the period.

He wrote to the Tzar on 10 May 1887, "Before I take the liberty of placing before His Majesty's Government the request of the princes and people of India for their deliverance from their oppressors, I wish to say that I seek no personal advantage for my self. I only desire the freedom of 250,000,000 of my people from the British tyrants and thus also benefit the persons who will free them... One thing alone I wish to have, when the people of India become free, I wish to live in my own country in the Punjab from where the British have expelled me.... Through my near relation Sardar Thakar Singh who is well known in Punjab and in India, I was asked by most of the princes of India to go to Russia and request the Emperor's Government to take this word to hand. Those princes have altogether an army of 300,000 and are ready to fight when the Imperial Government have decided to attack British Empire in India. I should like to accompany the army and show it to my people how kind and generous His Majesty has been to us... It will not be out of place here to explain why I have such influence on my people and can do appreciable work for the Imperial Government. I am the king of 22 million people out of which 8 million belong to the martial race; in other words the whole of Punjab which is inhabited by the most warlike people in India and they are all ready for me.... It is not my business to interfere in the question whether the Imperial Government is to invade India or not. I am only acting as the agent of 250 million of my people for freeing them from British slavery. In doing so I am only discharging my duty...."[50]

The above letter was duly received by the Russian King who gave his comments on the letter which showed his inclination towards the subject but were not obvious of the intentions. The Maharaja was not granted interview with the Tzar. The Maharaja did not relent. He wrote letters to France, Germany, Austria, Sudan and Turkey and sent these through his emissary Abdul Rasul Kashmiri. The first three states did not respond stating that the Maharaja had no active support in his own country. However, the anti-British party led by Zubair Pasha, the Ex-Prime Minister of Sudan and Ahmad Mukhtar Pasha, a Minister of the Turkish Government assured the Kashmiri emissary of their active and fruitful support to the Maharaja asserting that they would close the Suez Canal as soon as there would be rising in the Punjab. Even Sikandar Khan of Herat and Ali Khanoff, the Governor of Panjdeh, had shown keen interest in the plan. People in Punjab were enthusiastic of the plans as they got the news from different sources. Mahan Singh, Sawan Singh, the two Kuka representatives started for Russia to meet the Maharaja. A party from Jullunder consisting of Sunder Singh, Sandoor Singh and Baba Bandri were spotted at Mashed. Moti, forty years old Jhiwar from Gurdaspur, was also on way to Russia for the same purpose, who when arrested, committed suicide.

The Maharaja wrote letters with his plan to the Indian princes asking them to rise against the British. Two letters, one to Raja of Indore and another to the deposed Nawab of Oudh, Nawab Wajid Ali, with a separate general appeal to all other Indian Princes to send assistance to the Tzar of Russia was despatched by him in May 1887 through his confidant Aroor Singh. Aroor Singh was however arrested by the British CID on 5th August 1887 on the third day of his arrival at Calcutta. These valuable documents were captured from his person by the British officials.

Blows that Broke the Heart

The Russian friend Katkoff became dangerously ill in July 1887 and died next month. Thakur Singh Sandhanwalia also died in the same month i.e., on 18 August 1887. These events of the month of August 1887 were great blows which broke the heart of the Maharaja who was now left to face the situation alone. His very important contact Abdul Rasul Kashmiri who started from Moscow with the Maharaja's messages too was arrested in January 1890 when

137

he reached Bombay.

The British had taken very stringent measures and got proclamations from the leading Sardars of Punjab against the Maharaja. The British CID closed all doors for him. Added by the deaths of his close friends and associates and arrest of his emissaries and no clear support coming from any source the Maharaja started back to France in May 1888 through Kiev and reached Paris on 3rd November 1888. Returning from Russia to Paris, Duleep Singh had a stroke and remained bedridden for three years. Drained financially and destitute of friends, he died in his humble hotel room in Paris on 22 October 1893. His body was taken to Elveden, England, by his son Prince Victor, where it was interred besides the graves of Prince Fredrick and Prince Edwards.[52] The relentless crusader did not get peace in the foreign land even after his death and might be looking towards his countrymen to get back to his home.

Col. (Dr.) Dalvindar Singh

References

1. Harbans Singh   *The Encyclopaedia of Sikhism*, Vol I, Patiala, Punjabi University, 1995, p. 599

2. Ibid.

3. Ganda Singh   'Maharani Jind Kaur of Lahore and her Letters' *The Punjab Past and Present*, Vol X, Part I, April 1976, Patiala, Punjabi University, p. 65

4. Ibid.

5. Avtar Singh Gill   'Maharaja Duleep Singh, The Relentless Crusader' *Maharaja Duleep Singh* Ed, Prithipal Singh Kapur, Amritsar, SGPC, 1996, p. 37

6. Gurdial Singh Grewal   *Freedom Struggle of India*, Ludhiana, Sant Ishar Singh Rarewala Education Trust, 1991, p. 33

7. Talwar K.S.   'Early Phases of Sikh Renaissance and Struggle for Freedom' *The Punjab Past and Present*, Vol IV, Part II, Oct. 1970, p. 188

8. Harbans Singh   Op. Cit. p. 600

9. Ibid.

10. Ahluwalia M.L. & Kirpal Singh   *The Punjab's Pioneer Freedom Fighters*, Orient Longmans, 1963, p. 87

11. Lady Login — *Lady Login's Recollections*, Patiala, Language Deptt., Punjab, p. 88

12. Ahluwalia, M.L. & Kirpal Singh — *The Punjab's Pioneer Freedom Fighters*, p. 87.

13. Surinder Kaur Anand — 'Maharaja Duleep Singh. A Psychoanalytical Study' *Maharaja Duleep Singh*, p. 83

14. Krishan Lal Sachdeva — 'Duleep Singh seeking Russian Support for Liberation of India (1887-88)' in *Maharaja Duleep Singh*, p. 117

15. Gian Singh Giani — *Twareekh Guru Khalsa*, Patiala, Bhasha Vibhag Punjab, 1987, p. 539

16. Avtar Singh Gill — Op. cit. p40-1

17. Evans Bell — *The Annexation of Punjab and Maharaja Duleep Singh*, pp. 92-96

18. Lady Login — *Recollections*

19. Grewal D.S. — 'Nasik vich Sikh Itihas dian Nishanian' *Punjabi Digest*, New Delhi, Sept. 1995

20. Harbans Singh — Op. cit. p. 600

21. Ibid.

22. Avtar Singh Gill — Op. cit. p. 45

23. Ibid, p. 46

24. Ganda Singh — *History of freedom Movement in the Punjab— Maharaja Duleep Singh's Correspondences*, Patiala, Punjabi University, 1962, p. 207-8.

25. Harbans Singh — Op. cit. p. 601

26. Ahluwalia M.L. & Kirpal Singh — *The Punjab's Pioneer Freedom Fighters*, p. 87

27. Avtar Singh Gill — Op. cit. p. 49

28. Op. cit. p. 48

29. Michael Alexander & Sushila Anand — *Queen Victoria's Maharaja Duleep Singh, 1838-93*, p. 190

30. Ganda Singh(Ed.) — Op. cit. p. 361

31. Op. cit. 226-7

32. Thapar K.S. — 'Maharaja Dalip Singh at Aden', *Journal of Sikh Studies*, Vol. II, No. 2 August 1975, p. 133

33. Michael Alexander & Sushila Anand — Op. cit.

139

34. Ganda Singh(Ed.)   Op. cit.
35. Op. cit. p. 226-7
36. Gian Singh Giani   *Twareekh Guru Khalsa*, Vol. II, p. 539
37. Harbans Singh   Op. cit. p. 601
38. Ibid.
39. Ibid.
40. Ganda Singh(Ed)   Op. cit. p. 361
41. Langer William   *European Alliances and Alignments*, Vintage Books, New York, 1950
42. Florinsky Michael T. *Russia: A History & Interpretation Vol. II*, The McMillan, New York, 1964
43. Thapar K.S.   'From the Russian Archives Papers relating to Maharaja Dalip Singh, *Journal of Sikh Studies*, Vol IV, No. 1, Feb 1977, Amritsar, GND University, p. 75
44. Jagjit Singh (Dr.)   Maharaja Duleep Singh, typed copy, p. 55
45. Avtar Singh Gill   Op. cit. p. 50
46. Ganda Singh   Op. cit.
47. Harbans Singh   Op. cit. p. 601-2
48. Avtar Singh Gill   Op. cit. p. 50
49. Harbans Singh   Op. cit. p. 602
50. Thapar K.S.   *Journal of Sikh Studies*, Vol IV, No. 1 Feb, 1977, p. 83-84
51. Harbans Singh   Op. cit.

Chapter VI

COINAGE DURING THE PERIOD OF MAHARAJA DULEEP SINGH

Numismatics—the study of coins—has always played a vital role not only in ascertaining historical facts, but also in discovering previously unknown rulers, their kingdoms and their influences. In some cases, even the history of a particular dynasty is largely based upon its coinage. For example, a detailed study of the coins of the Naga Kings of Padmavati by Shri H.V.Trivedi helped him to identify and discover several hitherto unknown and undiscovered Naga Kings.

Numismatics has also been helpful in determining the influence of different rulers at different times at different places. Sometimes a new find in numismatics changes the whole perspective of existing beliefs. On the other hand, sometimes, lack of actual numismatic evidence has led to much speculation and a lot of controversy. A classic example is that of Hari Singhee coins supposedly got minted by Hari Singh Nalwa in his own name during his governorship of Kashmir. One has still to come across such a coin. But still many historians are of the firm conviction that such coins did exist.

Most of the study in numismatics by historians, it appears, is based not much upon the actual study of the coins but upon the work done by others. Numismatics offers a first hand information of the historical facts, and provides an opportunity to present history without distortions and as much close to reality as possible. Very few attempts have been made to study numismatics as supportive evidence of contemporary history. Its interaction with history has often been neglected.

Sikh numismatics i.e. the study of the coins of the Sikhs, despite certain limitations, has been very helpful in ascertaining the influence of the Sikhs and Sikh rulers in various regions of the Punjab at different times. The words "Sikh" and "Sikh rulers" have required a separate mention because even before the establishment of the Sikh Kingdom by Maharaja Ranjit Singh, the Sikhs held sway over the vast territories of the Punjab in the form of several *Misls* or sometimes as petty local chiefs who had minted their own coins. Since the history of the Sikhs is very recent, events of the period have been well-documented by various authors, mainly historians and adventurers. In particular, the period of Maharaja Ranjit Singh and his successors has received special attention. But, unfortunately, the numismatics aspect of the Sikh history has been overlooked, if not neglected, by those engaged in the study of this period. No proper records of various mints and their methods of working are available. This has led to much speculation about the origin of different types of coins and different marks on them.

The best aspect of Sikh numismatics, vis-a-vis contemporary rulers in other parts of India, is that virtually all silver coins minted at different mints bear the year of issue very clearly in Vikrami Samvat[1]. Because of this, the coins pertaining to the period of Maharaja Duleep Singh can be easily identified and classified. These coins have some peculiar and interesting features of their own.

As we know, Maharaja Duleep Singh was enthroned as the ruler of Punjab in September, 1843 (VS 1900), following a bloody trail of events. At that time he was barely 5 years old. The coins issued from September, 1843 till the date of annexation of Punjab by the British on 20th March, 1849 are attributed to the period of Maharaja Duleep Singh. Whereas legibility of the year of issue of the coins is a positive aspect of the Sikh silver coins, a major draw-back has been that there has been no perceptible change in the type, design and pattern of these coins over the years. Since putting one's own name on a coin was considered against Sikh religious tenets, almost all Sikh coins in silver, minted at Lahore, Amritsar or Multan were Nanakshahis[2] or Gobind Shahis[3]. Due to this, coins of a particular year could not be ascribed with conviction to a particular ruler, especially during transition of power from one ruler to the other, as it happened between AD 1839, the year Maharaja Ranjit Singh died, and 1843, the year Maharaja Duleep Singh was enthroned as the ruler of Punjab. During these four years as many as four rulers figure as rulers of Punjab. The coins of all these years are available, but still cannot be attributed to an individual ruler.

However, coins minted between AD 1844 (VS 1901) and AD 1849 (VS 1906) can be safely attributed to the reign of Maharaja Duleep Singh. Only the coins of AD 1843 (VS 1900) retain an ambiguous position. Whereas prior to the assassination of Sher Singh in 1843 the coins bearing the year VS 1900 (AD 1843) should be attributed to the period of Sher Singh, the coins bearing the same year VS 1900, and in currency between September to December, 1843, have to be attributed to Maharaja Duleep Singh's period. Since the same coins remained in currency even during the transition of power from Maharaja Sher Singh to Maharaja Duleep Singh, a border line cannot be drawn as to which coin belongs to each of the two. This is also indicative of the smooth organisation and high efficacy of the mints, which continued to mint coins uninterrupted even when Punjab was in a state of turmoil.

Mints of the Period

Almost all the mints which had been working during Maharaja Ranjit Singh's period continued to mint the coins during Maharaja Duleep Singh's period. The only exception was the Peshawar mint, of which no coin is in evidence after VS 1894 (AD 1837).

The year on the reverse of the coins from Amritsar and Lahore mints is found to be frozen since VS 1884 (AD 1827) and VS 1885 (AD 1828). The actual year in which a coin was struck is found on the obverse in very small and inconspicuous, but distinctly legible, digits. Many explanations have been put forward to explain the reason for this. But the most plausible explanation appears to be that Maharaja Ranjit Singh fell seriously ill in AD 1827, and the illness got prolonged. Maharaja Ranjit Singh was a highly superstitious man. His astrologers advised him that by freezing the year on his coins he could stop time and thereby attain longevity. In light of this fact, the explanation holds good enough. But it is difficult to explain why this practice continued even after the death of Maharaja Ranjit Singh till the end of Sikh Rule i.e. the day of annexation of Punjab by the British in A.D. 1849.

143

When we talk about the coinage of Maharaja Duleep Singh's period, we should bear in mind that Duleep Singh was barely 5 years old when he was installed as the ruler of Punjab. It was his mother Rani Jindan who, as his regent, looked after the state of affairs. The study of the coins of the period suggests that no appreciable change in the type and design of the coins of Lahore, Amritsar and Kashmir mints was affected during that period. The following are the broad outlines/details of the coins of the various mints.

1. Amritsar Mint : Most of the silver coins of the Amritsar mint are still found in very good condition—rather uncirculated condition. This has led historians and numismatists to speculate that the coins minted at Amritsar were mainly used for religious/ ceremonial purposes, rather than for trade. In any case silver rupees minted between AD 1843 (VS 1900) to AD 1849 (VS 1906) are basically continuation of the frozen year series. The Nanakshahis have VS 1885 as the frozen year on the reverse, and VS 1900, 1901, 1902, 1903, 1904 as the year in which the coins were actually struck on the obverse, in inconspicuous lettering. The Gobindshahis have VS 1884 (AD 1827) as the frozen year on the reverse, and VS 1900, 1901, 1902, 1903 and 1904 on the obverse. There appears to be no rupee coin minted by the Amritsar mint in VS 1906 (AD 1849), the last year of Maharaja Duleep Singh's period. Also, no Gobindshahi coin is in evidence of the year VS 1905 (AD 1848) from Amritsar mint.

Nanakshahi 1/2 rupee is in evidence from VS 1900 to 1905 (AD 1843 to 1848), 1/4 rupee of VS 1901 to 1904 (AD 1844 to 1847) is known, 1/8 rupee of VS 1900 and 1903 is also known. All these fractional coins are with frozen year VS 1885.

There appears to be at least one serious attempt of providing an individual identity to the coins of Maharaja Duleep Singh's period by Amritsar mint in the year AD 1847 (VS 1904). Only one type of Gobindshahi silver coins struck with frozen year VS 1888 (AD 1831) on the reverse was minted in VS 1904 (AD 1847). This provides a special identity to the period of Maharaja Duleep Singh through coins. Again, in retrospect, this coin could have been minted elsewhere with mint name, Amritsar. Copper coins of

144

Amritsar mint that can be specifically attributed to Maharaja Duleep Singh's period are not in evidence. It is possible that copper coins during this period continued with the frozen year VS 1885, because although the year VS 1885 remained frozen, the mint marks found on these coins resemble with those found on silver coins of VS 1900 to 1903. However, coins of VS 1900 and 1901 are in evidence. These copper coins bear legend in Urdu on one side, and in Gurmukhi on the other side. Numismatists are not certain whether these belong to Amritsar mint or Lahore mint (Mr. S.P. Bhandari, a numismatist of repute, is convinced that these belong to Amritsar mint. He showed me the rubbing of a coin in his collection whereby the mint was partly but clearly, legible as Amritsar in Punjabi).

2. Lahore Mint : Silver rupees of Lahore mint continued in the same type and style as those during the period of Maharaja Ranjit Singh, and even prior to it. These have Nanakshahi couplet on the obverse with the year, in which struck, given inconspicuously. On the reverse is the frozen year VS 1885. The only coins known to be in evidence are of the year VS 1902 and VS 1903 (AD 1845 and 1846, respectively). It is significant to note that there is no coin of Lahore mint in evidence after VS 1903 (AD 1846). We know that the British regency at Lahore took over the affairs of state in December 1846. It is very much possible that they either discouraged or disallowed minting of new coins at Lahore.

Copper coins from Lahore mint are not individually distinguishable as to be related to any particular period. No particular coin can be assigned to Maharaja Duleep Singh's period. Not that copper coins were not minted during this period, but, apparently no attempt was made to provide them a separate identity.

3. Kashmir Mint : Silver coins minted in Kashmir have a distinction of having individual mint marks of most of the governors from Diwan Kirpa Ram in VS 1883 (AD 1826) onwards. During VS 1900 (AD 1843) to VS 1902 (AD 1845) Sheikh Ghulam Mohyi-ud-din was the governor of Kashmir. During VS 1902 (AD 1845), VS 1903 (AD 1846), Sheikh Iman-ud-din, Amir-ud-Mulk Bahadur was the governor of Kashmir. Silver coins during the tenure of these two governors are identified by an Urdu alphabet letter : " شن " (Shn) mark on them. Significantly in this case also there are no silver coins known to exist after AD 1846 (VS 1903). It is well known that in March 1846, Kashmir was handed over to Gulab Singh by the British as a reward for his treacherous role in the Sikh wars. In case of copper coins of Kashmir, there are none in evidence which can be attributed to Maharaja Duleep Singh's period with conviction. Not that copper coins were not minted during that period. But unfortunately, it appears, no attempt was made to provide them an identity of their own to enable us to relate them to Duleep Singh's period.

4. Multan Mint : During the reign of Maharaja Duleep Singh in Punjab, Multan was moving through a highly turbulent period. Sawan Mal, who was appointed the governor of Multan in 1829 by Maharaja Ranjit Singh, got assassinated in 1844, his son Diwan Mulraj succeeded him. He objected to the huge amount of 'nazrana' demanded by the British regency in lieu of confirmation of his succession. Two British missionaries along with governor designate Kahan Singh were assassinated at Idgah of Multan. Mulraj rewarded the murderers and rebelled against the British. This gave an excuse to the British to attack Multan and convert this local revolt into a war against the state and thus annex Punjab. Multan was invested by British forces in September, 1848 and stormed on January, 1849. Mulraj surrendered.

The purpose of the above narration is to convey to the reader that any coins minted during this period from Multan mint were totally independent from British influence. The silver rupees of Multan mint are known to exist for the years VS 1900 to 1905 (AD 1843 to 1848). These have Nanakshahi couplet on the obverse and the legend ZARB DAR AL-AMAN MULTAN JULUS MAIMANAT MANUS (struck at Multan, the abode of safety, in the year...... of the prosperous reign). The reverse carries the year in which struck. Fractional coins (i.e. 1/2 rupee or 1/4 rupee) may have been minted, but are not in evidence for the years of Maharaja Duleep Singh's period. Copper paisa of the year VS 1904 is in evidence. This is also a Nanakshahi coin with the Nanakshahi couplet on the obverse.

5. Dera Mint : Dera refers to Dera Ghazi Khan. Silver rupees of Dera mint are extremely rare. These have still not been deciphered convincingly. These rupees bear frozen year VS 1884 on the reverse and another year on the obverse. The years which have been read on the obverse are VS 1894 [Rupee from the collection of Saran Singh]; VS (1904) [Rodger's Leiah Rupee] and VS (1904) [Rodger's Dera Rupee), the digits given in small brackets are absent; therefore, only 4 is found on each of these. Could we have the liberty to speculate that the year on all these refers to VS 1904 (zero missing on Saran Singh's rupee being illegible)? Since Dera Ghazi Khan together with Mankera was a part of Multan, it is possible that in VS 1904 (AD 1847) Diwan Mulraj started a mint there to strengthen his rebellion against the British. No other coin of Dera mint is known to be in evidence.

6. Derajat Mint : Derajat or Dera Ismail Khan was the name given to alluvial plain with Dera Ismail Khan in the north, Dera Fateh Khan in the centre and Dera Ghazi Khan in the south, bordered in the east by river Indus and by Sulaiman mountain range in the west.

Silver coins (rupees) minted in Derajat mint during Maharaja Duleep Singh's period are in evidence of the years VS 1900 to 1904 (AD 1843 to 1847). Rupee of VS 1905 (AD 1848) is also reported. The inscription is probably Gobindshahi, which is never more than partly legible, in several slightly varying arrangements on the obverse. The reverse has the year inscribed in VS with mint name in Persian legend.

Copper coins of Maharaja Duleep Singh's period are not in evidence. Even if these exist, they are still to be traced.

7. Namakshahi Mint : In my opinion, this must be the most important mint in relation to the period of Maharaja Duleep Singh. The reason for this assumption is that this mint has struck silver rupees of the years VS 1904 and 1905 (AD 1847 and 1848, respectively) only (till date silver rupees with only these two years are known). The obverse of these coins has a Nanakshahi couplet inscribed on it, similar to those of Amritsar mint. The reverse of the rupee is exactly similar to that of the Nanakshahi of the Amritsar mint except that in this case the name of the Zarb (mint) is read as "NAMAK" by most numismatists. The complete name of the mint has been suggested "NAMAK SHAHI" by some numismatists, but is still to be ascertained. In one of the coins of VS 1905, the letters ए म जी म appear on the obverse. Numismatists are still to say with conviction whether these letters are in the Gurmukhi script or in Dev Nagri script.

The literary meaning of the word "NAMAK" means salt. It has been suggested that these coins were probably minted in the salt range.

I have earlier said that these coins appear to be the most important silver rupees in relation to the period of Maharaja Duleep Singh. My assumption is based on the fact that during these two years (i.e. AD 1847 and AD 1848) the British regency was managing the affairs of Punjab. They could never have permitted new mints. This mint definitely has to be a product of the rebellious proceedings, then going on in certain parts of Punjab.

—**Gurpreet Singh**

NOTES

1. *VS or Vikrami Samvat.* AD year can be arrived at by substracting 57 from the VS.

2. *Nanakshahi*: Originally the couplet containing the following text in Persian was used on Nanakshahi coins: SIKKA ZAD BAR SIM'O ZAR FAZL SACHCHA SAHIB AST FATEH-E-GOBIND SINGH-E-SHAHAN TEG-E-NANAK WAHIB AST (Coins struck in silver and gold by the grace of the true lord; of the victory of Gobind, Lion of Kings, Nanak's sword is the provider). The same couplet was used with slight variation from time to time.

3. *Gobindshahi*: The couplet containing the following text in Persian was used on Gobindshahi coins with slight variations from one mint to the other and from one period to the other.

DEG TEGH O FATEH NUSRAT BE-DARANG

YAFT AZ NANK GURU GOBIND SINGH

(Abundance, power and victory, assistance without delay are the gifts of Nanak (and) Guru Gobind Singh).

148

SILVER COINS OF AMRITSAR MINT
(Maharaja Duleep Singh Period)

NANAKSHAHIS :

Obverse : Couplet with year in which struck inconspicuous but distinct.

Reverse : VS 1885 frozen
SRI AMRITSAR JI ZARB TAKHT AKAL BAKHT
JULUS MAIMANAT MANUS SANAH

Rupee : 11.0 - 11.2 g

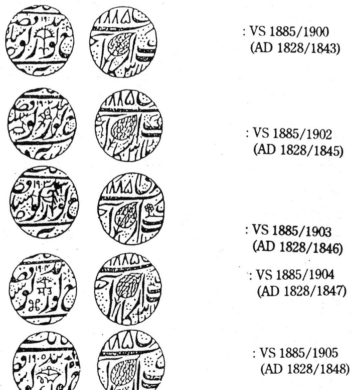

: VS 1885/1900
(AD 1828/1843)

: VS 1885/1902
(AD 1828/1845)

: VS 1885/1903
(AD 1828/1846)

: VS 1885/1904
(AD 1828/1847)

: VS 1885/1905
(AD 1828/1848)

OTHER YEARS ALSO REPORTED

½ Rupee : 5.5 - 5.6 g

: VS 1885/1900
(AD 1828/1843)

: VS 1885/1903
(AD 1828/1846)

OTHER YEARS ALSO REPORTED Sandhanwalia

¼ Rupee : 2.8 g

: VS 1885/1904
(AD 1828/1847)

OTHER YEARS ALSO REPORTED

MULTAN MINT
(Maharaja Duleep Singh Period)

SILVER RUPEE : 11.0 - 11.2 g

OBVERSE :
(NANAKSHAHI COUPLET)

REVERSE :

: VS 1900
  (AD 1843)

: VS 1905
  (AD 1848)

COINS OF THE YEARS VS 1901, 1902,
1903, 1904 ALSO KNOWN TO EXIST.

Annexture C

LAHORE MINT
(Maharaja Duleep Singh Period)

SILVER RUPEE : 10.9 - 11.1 g

OBVERSE :

      NANAKSHAHI COUPLET WITH YEAR IN WHICH
      STRUCK

REVERSE :

      VS 1885 FROZEN & MINT NAME

: VS 1885/1902
  (AD 1828/1845)

COINS OF OTHER YEARS ALSO KNOWN TO EXIST

Annexture D

DERA MINT
(DERA GHAZI KHAN)
(Maharaja Duleep Singh Period)

SILVER RUPEE : 11.0 - 11.1 g

OBVERSE :

GOBINDSHAHI COUPLET WITH YEAR IN
WHICH ACTUALLY STRUCK.

REVERSE :

AS AMRITSAR MINT BUT WITH MINT NAME
'DERA' 1885 FROZEN

      : VS 1884/94
     (AD 1827/....)

(SARAN SINGH'S COLLECTION RUPEE)

      :VS 1884/.4
     (AD 1827/....)

(RODGER'S COLLECTION RUPEE)

153

NIMAK MINT (?)

SILVER RUPEE : 11.1 g

OBVERSE :

NANAKSHAHI COUPLET

REVERSE :

SAME AS NANAKSHAHI OF AMRITSAR BUT
WITH MINT NAME SUPPOSEDLY 'NIMAK'

:VS 1905
(AD 1848)

: VS 1905
(AD 1848)

ADDITIONAL INSCRIPTION PROBABLY IN HINDI

Appendix I

BHYROWAL TREATY , 1846

Articles of Agreement concluded between the BRITISH GOVERNMENT and the LAHORE DURBAR, on Dec. 16th, 1846.

Whereas the Lahore Durbar and the principal Chiefs and Sirdars of the State have in express terms communicated to the British Government their anxious desire that the Governor-General should give his aid and assistance to maintain the administration of the Lahore State, during the minority of Maharaja Duleep Singh, and have declared this measure to be indispensable for the maintenance of the Government : And, whereas the Governor-General has, under certain conditions, consented to give the aid and assistance solicited; the following Articles of Agreement, in modification of the Articles of Agreement executed at Lahore on the 11th of March last, have been concluded on the part of the British Government by Frederick Currie, Esq., Secretary to the Government of India, and Lieutenant-Colonel Henry Montgomery Lawrence, C.B., Agent to the Governor-General, North-West Frontier, by virtue of full powers to that effect vested in them by the Right Honourable Viscount Hardinge, G.C.B., Governor-General; and, on the part of His Highness Maharaja Duleep Singh, by Sirdar Tej Singh, Sirdar Shere Singh, Dewan Deena Nath, Fakeer Nooroodeen, Rae Kishen Chund, Sirdar Runjore Singh Mujeetheea, Sirdar Shumshere Singh, Sirdar Lal Singh Morareea, Sirdar Kher Singh Sindhanwala, Sirdar Urjun Singh Rungnungaleea, acting with the unanimous consent and concurrence of the Chiefs and Sirdars of the State assembled at Lahore.

Article I.—All and every part of the Treaty of Peace between the British Government and the State of Lahore, bearing date the 9th day of March, 1846, except in so far as it may be temporarily modified in respect to Clause 15 of the said Treaty by this engagement, shall remain binding upon the two Governments.

Aritcle II.—A British officer, with an efficient establishment of assistance, shall be appointed by the Governor-General to remain at Lahore, which officer shall have full authority to direct and control all matters in every department of the State.

Article III.—Every attention shall be paid, in conducting the administration, to the feelings of the people, to preserving the national institutions and customs, and to maintain the just rights of all classes.

Article IV.—Changes in the mode and details of administration shall not be made, except when found necessary for effecting the objects set forth in the foregoing clause, and for securing the just dues of the Lahore Government. These details shall be conducted by native officers, as at present, who shall be appointed and superintended by a Council of Regency, composed of leading Chiefs and Sirdars, acting under the control and guidance of the British Resident.

Article V.—The following persons shall, in the first instance, constitute the Council of Regency—viz., Sirdar Tej Singh, Sirdar Shere Singh Attarewala, Dewan Deena Nath, Fakeer Nooroodeen, Sirdar Runjore Singh Majeetheea, Bhaee Nidham Singh, Sirdar Utter Singh Kaleewala, Sirdar Shumshere Singh Sindhanwala; and no change shall be made in the persons thus nominated without the consent of the British resident, acting under the orders of the Governor-General.

Article VI.—The administration of the country shall be conducted by this Council of Regency in such manner as may be determined by themselves, in consultation with the British Resident, who shall have full authority to direct and control the duties of every department.

Article VII.—A British force of such strength and numbers, and in such positions as the Governor-General may think fit, shall remain at Lahore for the protection of the Maharajah and the preservation of the peace of the country.

Article VIII.—The Governor-General shall be at liberty to occupy with British soldiers any fort or military post in the Lahore territories, the occupation of which may be deemed necessary by the British Government for the security of the capital, or for maintaining the peace of the country.

Article IX.—The Lahore State shall pay to the British

Government twenty-two lakhs of new Nanuk Shahee rupees, of full tale and weight per annum, for the maintenance of this force, and to meet the expenses incurred by the British Government; such sum to be paid by two instalments, or thirteen lakhs and 20,000 in May or June, and eight lakhs and 80,000 in November or December of each year.

Article X.—Inasmuch as it is fitting that Her Highness, the Maharanee, the mother of Maharajah Duleep Singh, should have a proper provision made for the maintenance of herself and dependents, the sum of one lakh and 50,000 rupees shall be set apart annually for that purpose, and shall be at Her Highness's disposal.

Article XI.—The provisions of this engagement shall have effect during the minority of His Highness Maharajah Duleep Singh and shall cease and terminate on His Highness attaining the full age of sixteen years, or on the 4th of September of the year 1854, but it shall be competent to the Governor-General to cause the arrangement to cease at any period prior to the coming of age of His Highness, at which the Governor-General and the Lahore Durbar may be satisfied that the interposition of the British Government is no longer necessary for maintaining the Government of His Highness the Maharajah.

This Agreement, consisting of eleven Articles, was settled and executed at Lahore by the Officers and Chiefs and Sirdars above-named, on the 16th day of December, 1846.

F. Currie
H. M. Lawrence

Tej Singh	Bhaee Nidham Singh
Shere Singh	Sirdar Khan Singh
Dewan Deena Nath	Shumshere Singh
Fakeer Nooroodeen	Lal Singh Morareea
Rae Kishen Chund	Kher Singh
Runjore Singh	Urjun Singh
Utter Singh	

Appendix II

PRINCESS BAMBA COLLECTION

By Dr. F.A. Khan, Director Archaeology Dept., Pakistan

Pakistan Archaeology Department has published two very interesting books in the area of Sikh history; one, *Sikh Shrines in Pakistan* and the other, *The Princess Bamba Collection*. The first book carries history supported by photographs of the Sikh places of historical interest in Pakistan. In the second, we have a collection of paintings which were in the possession of Princess Bamba, daughter of Maharaja Duleep Singh and grand-daughter of Maharaja Ranjit Singh. Paintings carry the authorship of renowned artists of Maharaja Ranjit Singh's time. Most of the important paintings of the time had been taken away by Maharaja Duleep Singh to England in 1849, when he was sent in exile there. After his death this national treasure remained in the care of Princess Bamba. Princess Bamba married an English doctor by the name Sutherland but she, like her sisters and brothers, died issueless. She died in Lahore (Pakistan) on March 10, 1957. With her death the priceless art treasure, the last of Maharaja Ranjit Singh's gift to posterity, was feared to have been lost forever. But luckily Princess Bamba had left the paintings with a responsible friend of hers, Pir Karim Baksh Sapra, for safe custody just before her death. When this was discovered, the Pakistan Government lost no time in buying up these paintings and many other historically important items from the Pir and passed these on to its Archaeology Department. The book though carries only photocopies of the paintings yet they portray admirably well the majesty and splendour of Maharaja Ranjit Singh's court and the times. We are giving hereunder an article on the subject by Dr. F.A. Khan who is the Director of Pakistan Archaeology Department, in the hope it would interest the readers.

Piara Singh Data

Princess Bamba's art collection have just been procured by the Pakistan Government for its Archaeology Department. The Collection was Maharaja Ranjit Singh's property. Many of the art treasures of Maharaja Ranjit Singh were taken away by Maharaja Duleep Singh to England when Punjab was annexed and he was sent to England in exile. The paintings remained in the care of Princess Bamba after the death of Duleep Singh. The Princess died in 1957 in Lahore (Pakistan) without leaving a heir. Needless to say, the art treasure is very valuable historically as it throws light on the life and times of Maharaja Ranjit Singh, the court life of the Maharaja and the life-style and manners of the Princes.

Sikh religion had its birth in the 15th century renaissance. The Sikhs came into power in the Punjab and the north western region of the country in early nineteenth century.

Sikh religion was founded by Guru Nanak who was born in 1469 in Talwande (Pakistan), now called Nanakana Sahib. His greatest contribution was that he carried on a relentless crusade against differences between man and man on the basis of caste and religion. His message was that there was no Hindu, no Musalman. All were equal children of one God. From his successors and their activities one can guess how well spread were their following and powerful their teachings that we have over 130 sacred places in Pakistan which have associations with the succeeding Gurus. These places and memorials continue to relay the message of Guru Nanak to mankind for all time to come.

Guru Nanak stressed on a virtuous living. Truth is higher, higher still is truthful living, he said. He disregarded differences between one religion and the other. He was only a religious preacher. He took no interest in politics. But after him the Sikh Gurus crossed swords with the Mughal Kings. After Aurangzeb's death, the Sikhs under the leadership of their religious leaders captured Sirhind and Delhi. That is why the eighteenth century was known as the revolutionary century for Punjab. In 1708, Guru Gobind Singh, the tenth Guru, passed on the Guru Gaddi to Guru Granth Sahib, the sacred scripture of the Sikhs, and the Sikh Panth's leadership to a Pandit by the name Lachhman Das who later became famous in history as Banda Bahadur. Banda Bahadur, equipped with Guru Gobind Singh's Khalsa flag, Nagara and five arrows, marched from his southern hamlet to Punjab. He tried to bring about a change in Sikh mores and manners but in the process came in disfavour of Mata Sundri, wife of Guru Gobind Singh. He thus developed religious differences with the Sikh leadership which weakened his armed strength. Consequently, he fell an easy prey to the Mughal forces.

After the death of Banda Bahadur in 1716, Sikhs were a demoralised lot. Religious concerns of the Sikhs were however looked after by Mata Sundri with the able assistance of Bhai Mani Singh. But their power was fast crumbling. Jats and Marathas were growing in strength; in Rajasthan they were openly in revolt. In 1738, Nadir Shah and from 1748 to 1767 Ahmed Shah Abdali with their attacks destroyed the Mughal power. But their attacks proved not the least harmful to the Sikhs who grew in strength as the Mughal power waned. The Sikhs were quick to extend their sway from Rawalpindi to Jamuna and beyond. But the internal feuding among the Sikhs reinforced by the assertive power of the Dogras, Afghanis, Gorkhas, Marathas and the English did not let them find their feet.

During such turbulent times Maharaja Ranjit Singh, with his sagacity and foresight, succeeded in laying the foundation of a strong Sikh state in the north-west of Satluj at the beginning of the nineteenth century. His success was attributed to his armed strength and political sagacity. All Punjabis, without distinction of caste and creed, were welcome into the Maharaja's service and play their part. His army comprised of Sikhs, Gorkha, Punjabi Muslims, Pathans, European officers. All worked shoulder to shoulder for the glory of the Sikh state. At one time there were over three dozen European instructors training Maharaja Ranjit Singh's army in modern combat. There were also many European generals in the army. But, alas! none of the white officers fought on the side of the Sikhs during the Anglo-Sikh wars.

It were the Muslims who were given the vital charge of launching cannon fire attack in the battle. Besides, there were many wise Muslim Sardars in Ranjit Singh's service, notable among them being Fakir Syed Noor-ud-din and Fakir Syed Aziz-ud-din.

Maharaja Ranjit Singh died in 1839 without naming his successor. In the ensuing battle of succession, the first one to succeed in ascending to the throne was Prince Kharak Singh who died in 1840. After his death his son Nau Nihal Singh ascended the throne. In 1843, Prince Sher Singh was made the Maharaja. But all these Maharajas fell victims to the machinations of their adversaries and courtiers. In 1843, Maharaja Duleep Singh, who was then just about six years of age, ascended the throne and reigned under the regency of his mother Jinda.

Maharani Jinda was the daughter of S. Mana Singh Aulokh,

a Sardar of Chogavan. The two Anglo-Sikh wars destroyed the Sikh rule and the Punjab passed on into the hands of the English. On March 30, 1849 Maharaja Duleep Singh was put in the care of Sir John Login at Fatehgarh. After two years of growing up as ward of an Englishman young Maharaja Duleep Singh was pursuaded to convert to Christianity. He was then sent to England. A *jageer* was given to him in Saphok. He married a certain young woman by the name, Bamba Muller, who was daughter of a European businessman. Her mother belonged to Abessynia.

Maharani Bamba could not speak or understand any language other than Arabic. Maharaja Duleep Singh had always great difficulty in understanding her and in being understood by her. She gave birth to three sons and three daughters including Princess Bamba. But all the children of Maharaja Duleep Singh died issueless. Maharaja Duleep Singh visited his motherland twice and got reconverted to Sikhism.

In 1886, he tried to leave England for good and settle down in Punjab but he was not allowed to do so. He was held up at Aden enroute to Punjab. Disappointed, he did not return to England but settled in Paris where he died in 1893.

Princess Bamba Jinda married an English doctor by the name Sutherland. After her father's death she became the proprietor of lot many historical paintings and other valuables which earlier belonged to her grandfather, Maharaja Ranjit Singh. She died on March, 10, 1957 in Lahore (Pakistan). She too like her other sisters and brothers had no issue. With her death, thus, Ranjit Singh's dynasty came to an end.

She left all these valuable paintings in the care of Pir Karim Baksh of Lahore who sold them to the Government of Pakistan.

The treasure trove of Princess Bamba, among others, include 18 oil paintings, 14 water paintings, 22 ivory paintings and 17 photographs. Most of these paintings are the works of European artists. Therefore these paintings do not belong to Punjab art genre, which was then dominated by Kangra School. Some paintings belonging to that period are available at the Central Museum, Lahore. Many paintings having association with the Sikh rule can be found in Ranjit Singh's memorial, in Naunihal Singh's Haveli (Lahore) and at the walls of the fort of Mir of Hyderabad.

Pakistan Archaeology Department has recently discovered many paintings having association with the Sikh Raj on the walls of the Lahore fort which had earlier been plastered during British rule.

Of the lot, four of the paintings are very important. Two of them depict Maharaja Ranjit Singh and Maharaja Sher Singh as presiding over the court in regal splendour. The third one throws light on their life. The fourth one features the Mughal King Bahadur Shah.

There is one painting which features Maharaja Duleep Singh. Maharaja Duleep Singh is the subject of a water colour painting also. This painting merits special attention. This is very interesting and captivating. Queen Victoria had commissioned a European artists Halter, to prepare it for display in her Buckingham Palace.

There are 22 ivory paintings which seem to have been inspired by the art form of the 19th century as in vogue then in Delhi, Agra and Banaras. Among this lot there are many historically important paintings featuring Maharaja Duleep Singh and the Princess.

Among the silver paintings, one that depicts Maharaja Ranjit Singh in royal dress mounted on an elephant (Length 32" width 23' and height 44') is simply remarkable. An engraved silver cup that was presented to Princess Sophia Duleep Singh is a valuable memento showing Sikh people's love for the royalty. From the book one can easily understand that the Persian language had a place of pride in the Sikh court.

In short, these paintings and many other mementos which have association with Maharaja Ranjit Singh's court, Maharaja Duleep Singh's exile in England and his bid to return to his motherland, are very valuable addition to the Pakistan's art treasure.

We are highly indebted to Pir Karim Baksh who had been good enough to take good care of these precious art treasure while in his safe keeping. It is his fervent desire that these treasures should not leave the soil of Pakistan.

Appendix III

BAMBA PALACE (LAHORE) AND ITS INMATE

Lahore is a town of Rajas, Maharajas, Nawabs, Pirs, Gurus and deities. Every inch of its soil has an imprint of history. The town has centuries-old temples, gurdwaras, churches, memorials of saints and tombs of kings, queens, princes and princesses. The story we are going to narrate today relates to a princess who lived stealthily, like an unknown stranger, in the capital of her own kingdom and quitely slipped into its soil unknown and unwept. Her name is Princess Bamba.

I learnt from a book that the last member of the Shere-e-Panjab Maharaja Ranjit Singh's family lived her last days in this very historical town—Lahore. Where did she live in Lahore? For how long she lived here? When did she breathe her last and where was her resting place? I could not find answers to these questions and had almost given up my search when one day, as chance would have it, I was in the midst of artists at the Studio of Pakistan Radio when I heard them indulging in reminiscences. They talked of Lahore of olden days, of kings and queens. Their reminiscences inevitably drifted to Maharaja Ranjit Singh, the last of the native kings of Lahore, Maharani Jind Kaur and then to their unlucky son Maharaja Dalip Singh and thence on to Princess Bamba, last of the Maharaja's descendants who, we were told, had lived in Lahore. That rekindled my interest and I was obliged by Panjabi Darbar programmer Khalida Arjum who provided all the answers to my questions. She proudly mentioned that her grandfather's brother's name was Pir Karim Bakhsh Sipra, a scholar and an historian and Godfather and Persian teacher of Princess Bamba. Karim Baksh was one man who had known the Princess from close quarters as long as she lived in Lahore. After her death Karim Baksh's family became the occupant of Bamba Palace which the Princess had built with so much care and fondness for herself.

History tells us that when the infamous court intrigues following the death of Maharaja Ranjit Singh had almost destroyed the Sikh Empire, its last hope was Maharaja Dalip Singh. But he had to become subservient to the British at a tender age. What to

163

speak of his kingdom, he had even to leave his motherland. The infant Dalip Singh was despatched to England on 19 April 1854. Here he flowered into youth and married a German girl, Bamba Muller, in 1864. He had three sons and three daughters from this marriage. The eldest son was named Prince Victor Dalip Singh who married a German girl from whom he got no issue. At the age of 52 he died. Next to him was Princess Bamba Jinda who was born on 29 September 1869 in London. Younger to her in line was Princess Catherine. In 1879 was born Prince Albert Edward Dalip Singh. He died in 1893 at the tender age of 13. Death of Prince Albert Edward hurt the Maharaja grievously and he died not long after, thousands of miles away from his kingdom and his beloved people. He died in Paris on 22 October, 1893. In 1874 another child was born to the Maharaja and was named Sophia Alexander. She lived long, for 74 years, breathing her last in 1948. Princesss Bamba was the last survivor of Maharaja Ranjit Singh's family.

Princess Bamba had one goal, an overriding passion with her, that somehow she must reach Punjab. She had great desire to see what was once the kingdom of her father and grandfather. Equally strong desire with her was to dispose off the ashes of her grandmother, Rani Jinda Kaur, according to her will. This was something that her father, despite every strategy he employed to get back to Punjab, had failed to do. The wise say rightly that slavery is after all slavery even if one is locked in a golden cage.

When she reached Lahore she lodged herself in the grandest of hotels in town—Flateez. After few days' stay in the hotel she got a bunglow on rent. She stayed over 2 years in this bunglow. During this period she advertised in the newspapers for a Persian teacher. Pir Karim Baksh was one of the candidates who tried their luck for the plum job.

The Princess found him a learned man and took no time to settle down to a happy working relationship. The Princess wanted to learn Persion so that she could read and understand her grandfather Maharaja Ranjit Singh's *Firmans* that he had issued during his rule. Shd did not like to show these historical documents to anyone and preferred to be able to read them by herself instead of having them read to her by someone else.

Pir Karim Baksh was a well-known scholar of Persian, Arabic and English. Very soon her relationship with her teacher became full of respect and trust.

One day she told the Pir that she wanted to buy a house for herself. Model town then was the most posh colony in Lahore. Gentry of this colony was in high-income and high-status bracket. She bought a beautiful house in this beautiful colony. She arranged to have a garden on all four sides of the house. She was very fond of roses. She had an exclusive garden of roses spread on an area of one *Kanal*. As you entered the central gate of the Palace there were roses and roses for as far as your eye could see. Even today though the palace is in a bad shape, roses are in plenty and ever in bloom waiting for their mistress.

The Princess lived in just one room of this spacious building. All her valuable possessions were also in the same very room. The facets of the Sikh Empire extending from Kabul to Delhi and its history were sitting jammed in the boxes in the room. In the boxes there were beautiful paintings of the Sikh Durbar, Royal edicts written in gold water, diamond-studded dresses and diamond necklesses and God knows what else there could be. It is said no one was allowed to enter this room except Pir Karim Baksh's wife. She alone was running errands for her and taking care of her comfort. She cooked for the Princess and accompanied her to the walks. Whenever she was called to the room she found diamonds and rubys spread on the floor. She collected and packed them but the next time again she found the jewels displayed likewise on the floor.

The Princess found her man while living in this very house. His name was Col. Sutherland. He was then the Principal of King Edward Medical College (now Medical University). He was a kind-hearted man, well-respected and known for his competance in his profession. But he did not live for long. The Princess was all alone once again though well-served, loved and cared by Pir Karim Baksh and his wife.

Her time had come too. She breathed her last on March 10, 1957. With her death the last of the survivors of Maharaja Ranjit Singh's family had passed away.

She was buried in the most beautiful, well-maintained cemetery of Lahore, the capital of her grandfather's sprawling empire. The cemetery lies in a posh colony by the name Gulbarg on the Jail Road that connects old Lahore with the new. The cemetery is known as Christian cemetery or white man's cemetery.

As you enter the cemetery and leave behind its office you walk about a 100 steps and on the left of the walk-way you would find a marble grave amid flowery bushes on which is engraved:

"The Princess Bamba Sutherland eldest daughter of Maharaja Dalip Singh and grand daughter of Maharaja Ranjit Singh of Lahore."

10 March, 1959

This is the grave of the daughter of Punjab's last native ruler. After the introduction as above, a little biographical data of the Princess, birth and death, etc. is etched, followed by a poem in Persian which serves as a prayer for eternal peace for her. The last words read:

This monument is erected secretary Pir Karim Baksh.

Whenever you visit this grave you will find heaps of red roses on it. These flowers come from Bamba Palace, 104-A, Model Town, Lahore. Even today the members of the Pir's family regularly every year pay homage to the Princess with flowers from her palace, which she herself had nursed.

Pir's sons and grandsons and grand-daughters have apportioned the palace among themselves. The Princess' treasures and other valuables have been deposited with the Lahore Museum and the Museum of the Royal Fort of Lahore. Rest of her belongings have been in the possession of Pir's sons and grandsons.

There is a part of the palace which always sports a lock and entry is obviously barred. But the lock is opened once a year, i.e. on March 10, the death anniversary of the Princess. When the lock is opened one gets access to the Princess' well-nursed rose garden. On March 10, flowers from the garden are plucked and laid on the grave of the Princess as the heart-felt homage.

(Based on Iqbal Kesari's report in a local newspaper)
—**Dr. Baldev Singh Baddan**

Appendix IV

"PUNJAB UNDER SIKH RULE...??"

Such were the headlines in Pakistani newspapers when Sardar Aarif Nakai became the chief minister of west Punjab in 1995. Sardar Aarif Nakai is the grandson of Ishar Singh who was the grandson of Gian Singh. Gian Singh was the head of one of 12 Sikhs *misls* called Nakai *misl.*

Between Lahore (Pakistan) and Gogira (India) lies the region of Nakka. For centuries this vast region has been peopled and dominated by Sandhu Jats. An elder of the Jat Sandhus by the name of Choudhri Hemraj, became the *Gursikh* of the fifth Guru of the Sikhs, Guru Arjan Dev. About a hundred years later one of his descendants S. Hira Singh founded the Nakai *Misl* which took its name from the region, Nakka. Later the *Misl* came into limelight when its head S. Gian Singh married off his sister Raj Kaur, alias Chand Kaur, to the youthful, rising Sirdar of the Sukerchakia *misl*, Ranjit Singh. Maharaja Ranjit Singh's successor, Maharaja Kharak Singh, was the son of this Nakian Queen.

So when S. Arif Nakai became the Chief Minister of Punjab (Pakistan) it was true indeed that the Chief Minister had Sikh ancestry and that Maharaja Ranjit Singh was Chief Minister's ancestor.

A section of S. Aarif Nakai ancestral family got converted to Islam in 1910. It was S. Ishwar Singh who converted to Islam and was rechristened as S. Abdul Aziz Nakai. Even after conversion the family continued to use Sardar and Nakai with their names.

S. Ishwar Singh Nakai alias S. Abdul Aziz Nakai's grandson S. Abdul Nakai is currently the head of the Nakai clan.

S. Aarif Nakai was born in Van Aadhin, a village close to Lahore. He owns about 2000 acres of land in the village. This looks like quite a lot of land and S. Aarif a big landlord, but in Pakistan where there are many landlords who own more than 10 lakh acres, S. Aarif can only be called a small landlord.

S. Aarif's political affliation is with Junejo group of the Muslim League. After the 1993 elections, while the centre was being ruled by Benazir Bhutto's Party (PPP) in Punjab there was a coalition between PPP and Muslim League (Junejo) under the Chief Ministership of Mian Manzoor Watto who belonged to the Muslim League (Junejo). But soon serious differences arose between the Chief Minister and his allies Pakistan Peoples Party with the result that Mian Watto's government was dismissed by the Governor. In 1995 S. Aarif Nakai who belonged to Muslim League (Junejo) was made the Chief Minister of the coalition Government, prompting newspapers and media to say that someone whose lineage can be traced to Maharaja Ranjit Singh is Punjab's new ruler.

(Based on a report in a local newspaper)

BIBLIOGRAPHY

Ahluwalia, M.L.	: *Maharaja Duleep Singh's Mission in Russia,* Proceedings of Punjab History Conference, 1965.
	: *Land Marks in Sikh History* (1699-1947), National Book Shop, Delhi, 1996.
Ahluwalia, M.L. and Kirpal Singh	: *The Punjab's Pioneer Freedom Fighters,* Orient Longman, 1963.
Ahluwalia, M.M.	: *Kuka—The Freedom Fighters of the Punjab,* Allied Publishers (P) Ltd., Bombay-1.
Aijazuddin, F.S.	: *Sikh Portraits by European Artists,* London, 1979.
Aitchison, Sir Charles	: *A Collection of Treaties, Engagements and Sanads Relating to India and Neighbouring Countries,* Calcutta, 1892.
	: *Lord Lawrence,* Rulers of India Series, Oxford, 1894.
Alberuni's India	: S. Chand & Co., Delhi, 1965.
Anand, Surinder Kaur	: 'Maharaja Duleep Singh, A Psychological Study' in *Maharaja Duleep Singh.*
Archer, W.G.	: *Paintings of the Sikhs,* London, 1966, Plates 61-62.
Arnold Edwin	: *The Marquis of Dalhousie's Administration of India, Vol. I & Vol. II,* London, 1862.
Ashok, Shamsher Singh	: *Jangnamah,* SGPC, Amritsar.
Baird, J.G.	: *Private Letters of the Marquis of Dalhousie,* London, 1911.
Bajwa, Fauja Singh	: *Kuka Movement,* Moti Lal Banarsi Das, Delhi, 1965.

Banerjee, Indubhusan : *Evolution of the Khalsa,* A Mukherjee & Co., Calcutta, 1963.

Baqir Muhammad : *Lahore—Past and Present,* Punjab University, Lahore, 1952.

Bhagat Singh : *Sikh Polity in the Eighteenth & Nineteenth Centuries,* Oriental Publishers, New Delhi, 1978.

Bhangu, Rattan Singh : *Prachin Panth Parkash,* Wazir-i-Hind Press, Amritsar, 1962 (4th ed.)

Bibliography—Sikh Studies, Vol. I, (Ed.) S.P. Gulati and Rajinder Singh, National Book Shop, Delhi, 1989

Bibliography—Sikh Studies, Vol. II., (Ed.) Dr. Jasmer Singh, National Book Shop, Delhi, 1993.

Bingley, A.H. : *The Sikhs,* National Book Shop, Delhi, 1985 (rpt.).

Bipan Chandra : *Struggle for Freedom,* Penguin, New Delhi, 1988.

Bosworth Smith, R. : *Life of Lord Lawrence,* Vols. I and II., Smith Elder & Co., London, 1883.

Calvert, H : *The Wealth and Welfare of the Punjab,* The Civil and Military Gazette, Lahore, 1936.

Catalogue of the International Art Exhibition of Maharaja Ranjit Singh: Deptt. of Archaeology and Museums, Punjab, (Delhi 1981).

Cooper, F.H. : *Crisis in the Punjab,* Lahore, 1859.

Cunningham, Joseph Davy : *A History of the Sikhs from the Origin of the Nation to the Battles of Sutlej,* London.

: *A History of the Sikhs,* S. Chand & Co., Delhi, 1955.

Dalip Singh	: *Guru Gobind Singh and Khalsa Discipline,* National Book Shop, Delhi, 1992.
Data, Piara Singh	: *The Sikh Empire (1708-1819 A.D.),* National Book Shop, Delhi, 1986.
	: *Maharaja Dalip Singh,* National Book Shop, Delhi, 1997 (rpt.).

Despatches and General Orders,
Announcing the Victories
achieved by the Army of the
Sutlej over the Sikh Army : National Book Shop, Delhi, (rpt.)

Dodwell, H.H.	: *The Cambridge History of India,* The University Press, Cambridge, 1932.
Douie, Sir James	: *Settlement Mannual,* The Civil and Military Gazette Press, Lahore.
Edwardes, Sir Herbert and Merivate Herman	: *Life of Sir Henry Lawrence,* London, 1892.
Edwardes, Herbert B. (Maj.)	: *A Year on the Punjab Frontier (1848-49),* National Book Shop, Delhi, (rpt.)
Eliot & Dowson	: *The History of India as Told by its Historians,* Kitab Mahal, Allahabad, 1961.

The Encyclopaedia of Sikhism
Vol. I	: Punjabi University, Patiala, 1995.
Evans Bell (Maj)	: *The Annexation of the Punjab & the Maharaja Duleep Singh,* National Book Shop, Delhi 1994 (rpt.).
Fitcheat, W.H.	: *The Tale of the Great Mutiny,* London, 1907.
Florinsky, Michael T.	: *Russia : A History and Interpretation,* Vol. II., The McMillan, New York, 1964.

171

Ganda Singh	: *Maharaja Duleep Singh's Correspondence*, Patiala, 1977.
	: *The British Occupation of the Punjab.*
	: *History of the Freedom Movement in Punjab; Maharaja Duleep Singh's Correspondence*, Punjabi University, Patiala, 1977.
	: Maharani Jind Kaur of Lahore and Her Letters. *The Punjab Past and Present*, Vol. X, Part I, Punjabi Univ., Patiala, 1976.
Giani Gian Singh	: *Twareekh Guru Khalsa*, Patiala Bhasha Vibhag, Punjab, 1987.
Gill Avtar Singh	: *Maharaja Duleep Singh, the Relentless Crusader*, SGPC, Amritsar 1996, Ed., Prithipal Singh Kapur.
Gill, Trilochan Singh	: *History of the Sikhs*, National Book Shop, Delhi, 1996.
Gopal Singh (Dr.)	: *History of the Sikh People.*
Gorden, Sir John J.H.	: *The Sikhs*, National Book Shop, Delhi, 1996 (rpt.).
Gough-Innes	: *Annexation of Punjab*, National Book Shop, Delhi, 1985 (rpt.).
Gough, (Gen.) Sir Charles and Arthur D. Innes	: *The Sikhs and the Sikh Wars*, National Book Shop, Delhi, 1984, (rpt.).
Grewal, J.S.	: *From Guru Nanak to Maharaja Ranjit Singh*, Guru Nanak Dev University, Amritsar, 1972.
	: *The Sikhs of the Punjab*, Cambridge University Press, Cambridge, 1990.
Grewal, J.S. and Indu Banga	: *Civil and Military Affairs of Maharaja Ranjit Singh*, National Book Shop, Delhi, 1988
Grewal, Gurdial Singh	: *Freedom Struggle of India*, Smt.

	Isher Singh Rarewala Education Trust, Ludhiana, 1991.
Grewal D.S.	: 'Nasik Vich Sikh Ithas Dian Nishanian,' *Punjabi Digest,* New Delhi, Sept. 1995.
Griffin, Lepel	: *The Punjab Chiefs* : Historical & Biographical Notes of the Principal Families in the Territories under Punjab Government, Lahore, 1865.
	: *Ranjit Singh,* Oxford, 1905.
	: *Rajas of the Punjab,* Language Deptt., Punjab, Patiala, 1970.
Gupta H.R. and Narang K.S.	: *History of the Punjab,* New Delhi, 1973.
Gupta, H.R.	: *Punjab on the Eve of 1st Sikh War,* Deptt. of History, Punjab University, Chandigarh.
Gurdev Singh (Ed.)	: *Perspectives on the Sikh Tradition,* National Book Shop, Delhi, 1996.
Harbans Singh	: *The Heritage of the Sikhs,* National Book Shop, Delhi, 1994.
Hasrat, B.J. (Dr.)	: *Anglo-Sikh Relations 1799-1849,* V.V. Research Institute, Book Agency, Hoshiarpur, 1968.
Henry Court (Maj.)	: *History of the Sikhs,* National Book Shop, Delhi, 1989 (rpt.)
Hunter, W.W.	: *The Marquis of Dalhousie,* Clarendon Press, Oxford, 1895.
Innes, A.D.	: *A short History of British India,* Mathew, London, 1923.
Jagjit Singh, Dr.	: *Maharaja Duleep Singh,* typed copy.
	: *The Sikh Revolution.*

Kahn Singh	: *Gurshabd Ratanakar,* 1997.
Kartar Singh	: *Guru Gobind Singh and the Mughals,* Guru Gobind Singh Foundation, Chandigarh, 1967.
Khilnani, N.M.	: *The Punjab Under the Lawrences,* Punjab Govt., Simla, 1951.
Khushwant Singh	: *A History of the Sikhs,* Princeton University Press, London, 1966.
Kirpal Singh (Dr.)	: *The Historical Study of Maharaja Ranjit Singh's Times,* National Book Shop, Delhi, 1994.
Kohli, Sita Ram	: *Sunset of the Sikh Empire.*
Kohli, Surindar Singh (Dr.)	: *The Sword and the Spirit,* National Book Shop, Delhi, 1990.

Lady Login	: *Sir John Login & Duleep Singh (rpt).* 1986, Lal Publishers, New Delhi.
	: *Recollections,* Language Deptt., Patiala.
Lafont, Jean Marie	: *French Administrators of Maharaja Ranjit Singh,* National Book Shop, Delhi, 1988.
Langer William	: *European Alliances and Alignments,* Vintage Books, New York, 1950.
Latif, Syed Mohammad	: *History of the Punjab from the Remotest Antiquity to the Present Time,* Calcutta, 1891.

Macauliffe, Max Arthur, (Ed.) S.P. Gulati	: Guru Hargobind, National Book Shop, Delhi, 1997.
Mackenzie, Helen (Mr. Colon)	: *Life in the Mission, the Camp and the Zenana or Six Years in India* (London 1853).
Majumdar, R.C.	: *History of the Freedom Movement in*

India, Vol. III, Firma K.L. Mukhopadhyaya, Calcutta, 1963.

Mansukhani, Gobind Singh (Dr.): *A Book of Sikh Studies.*

Mcleod, W.H. : *The Evolution of the Sikh Community,* Oxford University Press, London, 1975.

Michael Alexander and Sushila Anand : *Queen Victoria's Maharaja Duleep Singh,* Vikas Publishing House, New Delhi, 1980

Narang, Gokul Chand : *Transformation of Sikhism,* New Book Society of India, New Delhi, 1956.

Nayyar, G.S. : *Sikh Polity & Political Institutions,* New Delhi, 1979.

Niharranjan Ray : *The Sikh Gurus and the Sikh Society,* Punjabi University, Patiala, 1970.

Nijar, B.S. : *Punjab Under the British Rule 1849-1947,* K.B. Publications, Delhi, 1974.

Orlich L. Von : *Travels in India, including Sind and Punjab,* 1845.

Panikkar, K.M. : *A Survey of Indian History,* Asia Publishing House, Bombay, 1964.

Parrinder Geoffrey : *A Short History of the Sikhs,* Deptt. of Languages, Punjab, 1970 (rpt.).

Princip, Henry T. : *Origin of the Sikh Power in the Punjab and Political life of Maharaja Ranjit Singh (rpt.).* Language Deptt. Punjab. 1970 (First Pub. 1847)
Punjab Past & Present, Sr. No. 2, Vol. I & II, 1973.

175

Sachdeva, Krishan Lal : 'Duleep Singh Seeking Russian Support for Liberation of India (1887-88)' in *Maharaja Duleep Singh.*

Sachdeva Veena : *Polity & Economy in Late Eighteenth Century Punjab*, Manohar, New Delhi, 1991.

Scott, G.B. : *Religion and Short History of the Sikhs*, Language Deptt., Punjab, Patiala, 1970.

Sharma, Sri Ram : *Punjab in Ferment*, S. Chand & Co. (Pvt.) Ltd., New Delhi-1

Sharma Radha : *Peasantry under Sikh Rule* (1765-1849), Guru Nanak Dev University, Amritsar, 1988.

Sidhu, Kuldeep Singh, (Col.): *Ranjit Singh's Khalsa Raj and Attariwala Sardars*, National Book Shop, Delhi, 1994.

Sinha N.K. : *Rise of the Sikh Power*, Mukherjee & Co., Calcutta 1973 (Reprint).

Sita Ram Kohli : *Maharaja Ranjit Singh*, Delhi, 1953.

Suri, Sham Lal : *Umdet-Ut-Tawarikh*, Lahore, 1885-89, Guru Nanak Dev University, Amritsar, 1985.

Talwar K.S. : Early Phases of Sikh Renaissance and Struggle for Freedom, *The Punjab Past & Present* Vol. IV, Part II, Oct. 1970.

Tara Chand : *Influence of Islam on Indian Culture*, The Indian Press Publications, Allahabad, 1963.

Teja Singh and Ganda Singh : *Maharaja Ranjit Singh*, First Death Centenary Memorial, Patiala (rpt.).

Thackwell, Edv. Joseph : *The Second Sikh War*, National Book

176

Shop, Delhi, 1996 (rpt.). (Ed.) S.P. Gulati

Thapar K.S. : Maharaja Dalip Singh at Aden,
*Journal of Sikh Studies, Vol. II,
No. 2,* August 1975, *Journal of Sikh
Studies, Vol. IV, No. 1,* Feb. 1977,
G.N.D. University, Amritsar.

Toynbe Arnold J. : *A Study of History,* Oxford
University Press, London, 1971.

Trial of Diwan Mul Raj : Sita Ram Kohli (Ed.), National Book
Shop, Delhi, (rpt.).

Trial of Raja Lal Singh : R.R. Sethi (Ed.), National Book
Shop, Delhi, (rpt.).

Trotter, L.J. : *History of India,* Vol. I & Vol. II,
W.H. Allen & Co., Pall Mall,
London.

Waheed-Ud-Din, Fakir Syed : *The Real Ranjit Singh* (4th Ed.) Lion
Art Press, Karachi, 1965.

Periodicals
Asiatic Researches.
Indian Antiquary (I.A.).
Indian Historical Quarterly (I.H.Q.).
Journal of Asiatic Society.
Journal of Asiatic Society Bengal.
Journal of Bihar and Orissa Research Society.
Journal of Bombay Branch Royal Asiatic Society (J.B.B.R.A.S.).
Journal of Royal Asiatic Society (J.R.A.S.).
Journal of Royal Asiatic Society Bengal (J.R.A.S.B.).
Punjab Past and Present (Punjabi University, Patiala).
Punjab History Conference Proceedings (Punjabi University,
Patiala).

Books (Punjabi)
Batalvi, Ahmad Shah, *Tarikh-i-Punjab,* Trans. By Gurbax
Singh, Punjabi University, Patiala

	1969.
Bhangu Rattan Singh,	*Prachin Panth Prakash,* Edited by Vir Singh, Khalsa Samachar, Amritsar, 1962.
Ganda Singh,	*Amarnama,* Edited by Sikh History Society, Patiala, 1953.
	: *Hukamnama,* Punjabi University, Patiala, 1967.
	: *Gurbilas Cheevin Patshahi,* Anon, Bhasha Vibhag, Punjab, 1970.
Kannahiya Lal	: *Tarikh-i-Punjab,* Trans. by Jit Singh Seetal, Punjabi University, Patiala, 1968.
Karam Singh	: *Historian di Itahasik Khoj,* Edited by Heera Singh Dard, Shiromani Gurudwara Prabandhak Committee, Amritsar.
Kesar Singh, Chibbar	*Bansawalinama Dasam Patshahian Ka,* Punjabi University, Chandigarh, 1972.
Kishan Singh	: *Sikh Lehar,* Arsi Publishers, Delhi, 1971.
Koer Singh	: *Gurbilas Patshahi Das,* Punjabi University, Patiala, 1968.
Mehma Parkash	: Sarup Das Bhalla, Bhasha Vibhag, Punjab, 1978.
Prem Sumarag Granth,	Edited by Randhir Singh, New Book Co., Jullunder, 1965.
Sarabloh Granth,	Baba Santa Singh Jathedar Chianven Krori, Anandpur Sahib, Punjab.
Shahid Bilas,	Edited by Garja Singh, Punjabi Sahit Academy, Ludhiana, 1961.
Sujan Rai Bhandari	: *Khalastut Twarikh,* Punjabi University, Patiala.

INDEX

180

183